# HOW TO INFLUENCE PEOPLE AND GET WHAT YOU WANT NOW

*Become The Person Everybody Listens to by Mastering the Art of Influence & Manipulation. Learn How to Persuade Your Partner, Boss or Colleagues*

# Table of Contents

Introduction ........................................................................................................ 5

**Chapter 1: A Beginner's Guide to Persuasion** .................................................. 10
    *Everyday Ways You're Being Manipulated* ................................................... 10
    *Manipulation: A Tool for Both Good and Evil* ............................................. 11
    *6 Golden Rules of Manipulation* .................................................................. 13
    **How to Use Persuasive Body Language** ..................................................... 19

**Chapter 2: Emotional Intelligence 101** ............................................................ 23
    *What Is Emotional Intelligence?* ................................................................... 24
    *Why Master Manipulators Need Emotional Intelligence* ............................... 29
    *9 Ways to Develop Powerful Emotional Intelligence* ................................... 31
    *How to Control Your Emotions Like a Boss* ................................................ 36

**Chapter Three: Choosing Your Target** ........................................................... 41
    *What Hooks People In?* ................................................................................. 44
    *7 Qualities That Signify the Perfect Target* .................................................. 56
    *The Targets That are Harder to Win Over* .................................................... 58

**Chapter Four: Decoding Body Language** ....................................................... 61
    *Reading the Body's Subtle Signals* ............................................................... 61
    *The Secret Messages of the Face* .................................................................. 64
    *Understanding Microexpressions* .................................................................. 70
    *What Walking Styles Say About Someone* ................................................... 73

**Chapter Five: Essential Manipulation Tools** ................................................... 76
    *Everyday Manipulation Tricks* ...................................................................... 76
    **11 Persuasion Tricks to Start Getting What You Want in Everyday Life** ... 83
    *How to Use the Six Laws of Persuasion* ....................................................... 85
    *All You Need to Know About Reverse Psychology* ..................................... 88

**Chapter Six: A Master in Every Arena** ........................................................... 95

*How to Secretly Manipulate Your Boss* ............................................................... 95

*Killer Negotiation Strategies to Manipulate Your Way to Success* ................. 102

*Fractionation: The Seduction Tool of Master Manipulators* .......................... 106

*11 Less-Known Manipulation Techniques for Seduction* ................................ 112

**Chapter Seven: Advanced Manipulation Tactics** ............................................ 119

*The Manipulative Power of Reinforcement* ...................................................... 119

*Charming Habits to Manipulate Anyone* .......................................................... 123

*How to Turn Someone Into their Own Enemy* .................................................. 127

**Chapter Eight: Asserting Dominance** ............................................................... 131

*Body Language that Asserts Dominance* .......................................................... 131

*How to Talk Like a Top Dog* ............................................................................. 136

*Dominant Behavior to Show Who's Boss* ......................................................... 143

**Conclusion** ............................................................................................................ 148

# Introduction

Everyone has a little manipulator living inside of them. If you're feeling insecure about your life, it might be hard to recognize this quality and the power it can have over others. As humans, we have a wide variety of methods we instinctively fall back on when we want to exercise our influence over others. We might make people doubt their own judgment in lieu of our personal advice when we want something; we could make people feel guilty about something we don't like, or we might put on the charm to entice someone to do something they are reluctant to do. It's all part of daily communication and we start relying on it very early in life.

However, somewhere along the line, we become convinced that manipulation has somehow become immoral; that there is something inherently indecent about it and so they change their means of communication. Sadly, this leaves them vulnerable to the devices of those who recognize that the skill is merely a tool that can be used for both good and bad purposes. As a result, they find themselves being manipulated and pushed to do things they don't really want to do. They end up feeling powerless, frustrated, and out of control.

What they are failing to recognize is that manipulation, like any other craft, is a skill that can easily be developed and used in a positive way to help them achieve their goals. Just by making a few tweaks to their body language, speech, and behavior, all of us can position ourselves to become masters of our own lives. It doesn't matter if you're a parent trying to get your child to clean his room or the CEO of a major corporation trying to motivate a massive workforce, getting past your own insecurities and learning how to use this skill can change the whole dynamic of your life.

It has sometimes been referred to as a form of "dark persuasion" as if to imply that there is something mysteriously evil about manipulation. On the surface, it may seem like that is true. After all, when you hear the word 'manipulation' the mind automatically conjures up intriguing ideas. Visions of science fiction movies on mind control play out in your head, hypnotists attempting to get you to do strange or embarrassing things you wouldn't normally do, and unethical people who want to persuade you into some form of questionable acts. But these are all misconceptions of what manipulation is all about.

The most common belief about manipulation is that it involves one person taking control over another as if they were a puppet with them controlling the strings. But what most people are missing is that the true art of manipulation has nothing to do with getting people to do things against their will but is instead a gentle form of persuasion that will convince them to want the same thing that you want. In other words, manipulation is simply deep form of persuasion, something that all of us do in our everyday lives.

Your goal is to get others to believe that whatever action they are taking was actually their idea all along. While there are always going to be people who will use this skill for questionable purposes but doesn't mean that the art of persuasion itself is wrong.

A person can use a knife to prepare a meal for their family or they can use it to cause harm to someone else. The knife itself is not the problem, it is how someone chooses to use it. If you follow the media then you know that historically there have been an endless stream of charismatic people that have put forth a lot of effort to influence and maneuver people to do their bidding. They look to control the behaviors of the masses in subtle ways that may be difficult to notice.

All of us have heard of the horrific stories of the Nazi oppression of the Jews during World War II. How many normally peace loving and kind Germans were duped into believing that the Jews were really a threat to their way of life? Or you may have heard about the record number of suicidal deaths committed at the persuasion of charismatic people like Jim Jones or those that participated in the pact formed in the wake of the Hale-Bopp comet. Our history books are riddled with such horror stories that show just how evil and dangerous psychological manipulation can be. However, those cases are not the norm and do not reflect the reality of what the art of manipulation truly is.

All of us practice manipulation in some form or another. We do it every day and never give it a second thought. In fact, the main definition of the word 'to manipulate' is "to manage or influence with skill," in some process of treatment or performance."

Manipulation is not the evil itself; it is how it is used that can become questionable. Do you have a religion? Do you have a clique that you belong to? Were you ever a part of a fraternity? Or a member of an exclusive club? Did you follow the rules at school? Is there office politics where you work?

All of these things groups were formed and grown by using some level of manipulation. The members were giving you gentle pressure to follow a certain norm, to fit into certain expectations, and to please a certain group of people. You just didn't realize that you were being manipulated because you wanted to be a part of the picture.

But after reading this book, you can be on the other side of that equation. Gently pushing people in one direction or another. The tricks are all there in your mind and how you think. All of that may need to change and our goal is to help you to do that. In this book you will learn:

- What manipulation really is and how to recognize when you're being manipulated
- Non-verbal language you're always sending out to the rest of the world
- How you EQ (Emotional Quotient) plays a part
- How to find out if you're lacking in EQ and how to get it back
- What attracts most people
- How to identify a person vulnerable to manipulation
- How to read body language and micro-expressions
- How the way you walk tells people a lot
- How to stock up your manipulation toolbox
- And how to manipulate others like a real pro
- And so much more

The question you have to ask yourself is why are you here reading this book? What is your goal in learning how to manipulate people. Keep in mind that to effectively manipulate people it will take a serious commitment in time. You will have to be patient and cultivate your art. It may seem easy, but in order for the strategies used here, you must practice them until they feel natural and effortless. This kind of skill takes time to cultivate and involves overcoming your own mental barriers and creating a very specific mindset.

That involves a lot of work and commitment. However, once you have mastered this skill, you will be able to accomplish amazing things. It will be easier for your new business to gain traction and pull ahead of the competition. You will be able to get the kind of support you need to overcome any obstacle. You'll have access to a wide source of resources, and you'll be able to communicate and connect to the rest of the world on your terms.

If you've ever wondered how someone with just the clothes on his back can seem to take on the rest of the world and win, then you've witnessed first-hand the power of manipulation. You don't need a basket full of tools or a lot of tricks up your sleeve. Whether you're looking to convince your kids to make certain life choices or you're a CEO trying to motivate a team of employees to follow your ideals, the strategies are the same.

What does that mean for you? It means a lot. With the art of manipulation, you'll find it easier to get the job you want, get the types of loans you need, and even negotiate the kind of deals you're seeking. Your goal is not to get people to go against their will and help you, but to convince them that what you have to offer to the world is worth them taking a risk on. That's a powerful tool that anyone can use to get what they need. And it's all about learning how to use your own personal strengths to your advantage. So, if you're ready to take on the world and finally get the things you need and should have, then it's time to turn the page and learn to be a master manipulator in your own right. So, let's get you started so you can take the rest of the world by storm.

# Chapter 1: A Beginner's Guide to Persuasion

Most people think of manipulation very negatively. They feel that anyone that is manipulative has a malevolent purpose and can't be trusted. Unfortunately, this is at least partially true. There are definitely those out there who wish to do you harm or take advantage of anyone who gets in their path.

One of the reasons we often associate manipulation with negative intent is because we don't have the ability to look into someone's heart and determine what their true motive is. So, rather than thinking someone is genuinely complimenting you, the mind often becomes suspicious and will adopt the worst case scenario.

Everyday Ways You're Being Manipulated

It would be nice to feel that when we make our own decisions that we are doing it of our own accord, but that is rarely the case. We live very busy lives and as a result, we often defer to the influences of others and use them as a sort of a shortcut or as a guide to drawing our own conclusions about a given situation faster. For the most part, this can work well, but it is rarely the wisest course of action.

For example, you come home and turn on the TV news to hear the latest events going on in the world. You see a media photo of Prince Charles holding up his middle finger to someone in the crowd. People are outraged that someone in the royal family would adopt such an action in public and you agree. Are you being manipulated or is it a real news report. The image in the picture is clear so you join in the crowd and are incensed by the photograph and launch your own protest against an insensitive member of the royal family.

However, while this incident did actually happen, the media did not show the whole story. The same image taken from a different angle, shows that Prince Charles was actually holding up three fingers as if he was counting something while talking calmly with someone in the crowd. It was not the single middle finger and his gesture was completely innocent.

That major example of manipulation had millions of people weighing in on the state of the royal family before the truth was really revealed. However, all manipulation does not come out in such a public way. It can come on a smaller scale as well. Consider those people who act as if they are better than you. Perhaps they have a higher education, or they make more money than you. Some even act that way because of their family line. When they talk to you, they take on a condescending voice as if speaking with a child. Their facial expressions make it clear that they see you as inferior.

Does this strategy work? Only if you accept this behavior and go along with it. If you become nervous and jittery in their presence you are giving them signals that you agree and you do see them as superior to you. How you respond to that type of behavior will let you know if they are manipulating you or not.

Other manipulating strategies may be seen in a person's body language, tone of voice, or even in what they don't say (silent treatment for example). There is a myriad of ways that one can try to manipulate you. If you take the time, I'm sure you'll find countless forms of manipulation being played out with you every day. It's a perfectly normal strategy that we all us throughout our lives.

Manipulation: A Tool for Both Good and Evil

It is cases like these that make people question whether manipulation is ethically sound or not. The media is notorious for these kinds of tactics. They use photography, carefully worded phrases, and other clever tactics to persuade people to feel a certain way.

However, while the message they deliver has some degree of truth it is not always the whole truth. Because someone uses manipulation for bad doesn't mean it is all bad. A closer look at our communication styles helps us to understand how manipulation has been used far more for good purposes. Once you recognize this, you'll not only be able to recognize it when you see it playing out around you, but you'll want to apply it in your own life as well.

Because our subconscious mind is usually the force that is driving our behavior, we don't often recognize what is really happening during our mental processes. The subconscious mind is always at work, every second of every day, it is collecting information from our senses and putting it through filters, deciding what is important and what is not.

So, as you are scrolling through your computer, checking your social media pages, things are happening in the back of your mind that you're not even aware of. This is a strategy that marketers use to draw you in. A business' marketing team understands that if they put the brand name in front of you often enough, you'll eventually make a connection to it. Have you ever wondered why Coca-Cola has become the number one brand in the world of carbonated beverages? Little things like a catchy phrase, little blurbs in between scenes of your favorite TV show, and their logo plastered at every sports event and entertainment venue.

This crafty art of manipulation isn't something new. It has been around for decades. It is used by businesses, political parties, religions, and even social interest groups. Your employer uses it to get more work out of you, your parents use it to get you to come home by curfew, your teachers use it to get you to want to study, and your spouse may use it to get you to agree with him on any number of things. Simply put, manipulation is the skillful use of persuasion to achieve a desired result. It is the oil on the squeaky wheel that moves our society.

Bottom line, if you're a part of this world, you are in one of only two classes; the manipulator or the one being manipulated. There is no middle ground here. So, in essence, it is one of the most useful skills a survivalist can use to get what he needs.

If you're thinking that you need to have a special amount of charisma or certain talents to employ the strategies we will use in this book, then you'd be wrong. The fact is that everyone has an inborn talent to be a master manipulator. You already have the qualities to get the job done. So, let's start with the basics.

6 Golden Rules of Manipulation

So, how can you tell when you're being manipulated? There are a lot of ways this can happen. Chances are, by now you're starting to get the idea, but let's get a little more specific here. After years of study, researchers have narrowed down exactly how manipulation works.

In the beginning, you probably felt that people made decisions based on the information they have gathered, but that is not always the case. Evidence shows that manipulations has very specific characteristics and the decision-maker uses those characteristics as a kind of ruler to measure the information they collect. This allows them to come to a conclusion by bypassing all the analytical steps involved. There are at least six different rules of manipulation that are commonly used on you every day.

- Reciprocity
- Scarcity
- Authority
- Consistency
- Liking
- Consensus

Once you understand how each of these works and how they can be used you will not only be able to spot when someone is trying to manipulate you but will be able to harness this strategy and use it on others.

***Reciprocity:*** The art of reciprocity allows the manipulator to tap into an inborn characteristic of all of us. If someone does something for you, you automatically feel compelled to do something in return. Even if their gift does not come with an expectation in return, you will still feel as if you have to do something for that person before your mind will rest.

Still, don't expect it to be an equal exchange of gifts or favors. The manipulator may not even ask or expect something from you, but instead will create a situation that will make you feel connected to them in some way. Later, when the circumstances are favorable and they need the service or product you provide, your mind will automatically bring up their name and put it at the top of the list and the odds are good that you're going to throw your business their way.

A perfect example of reciprocity is a practice found in most restaurants today. After you've had your meal, the waiter will usually bring you the check along with a mint for each person in your party – a gift. In most cases, the gift is something small and seemingly insignificant. How do you feel when you receive this gift? What do you do? While the mint costs the restaurant a tiny fraction of the meal you just had, you begin to feel a sense of indebtedness. Your subconscious mind tells you that you have to return the gesture in some one. Evidence of this has been revealed in a number of studies that have shown that diners who receive a mint after their meal often increased the amount of their tip by at least 3%. If they received two mints, they size of the tip actually quadrupled to around 14%.

Another surprising result of reciprocity is if the waiter gives you a mint with the bill and then starts to walk away, pauses and then returns to compliment your party by saying something nice, the tips increase even more up as much as 23%.

This reveals something interesting. That it's not just the gift that makes a difference. Yes, giving a gift will increase your chances of getting what you want, but attention should also be paid to the manner in which the gift is given. This will give you the maximum possible results you receive.

*Scarcity:* It is a well-known fact that when there is only a limited supply of anything, people will want it more. This natural reaction is built into all of us. We may not even be aware of this inclination, but psychologically when something we desire becomes scarce, we feel compelled to try and get it as soon as possible.

We see how marketers use the art of scarcity in campaigns that have deadlines. You'll receive emails or text messages with phrases like "only 12 hours to go" or "just five seats left." To put it simply, once you realize that you no longer have infinite access to something you want you will be driven to take action and secure it for yourself before supplies are exhausted.

The important thing to remember here is that nothing has changed about the product. It isn't improved nor is it offered at a lower cost.

The only difference is that there is a good chance that the resource would no longer be available. That fact alone made people want it all the more.

So, when you really want to motivate people to action, the Principle of Scarcity is very effective. When people learn about the benefits they would be missing out on, they will be clamoring to get it while supplies last.

*Authority:* We have been programmed from a very young age to respect and accept the words and advice of people in authority. This is the reason we take the advice of medical professionals without question, we listen to the voice of a teacher, and we comply with the badge of authority whenever it gives us direction.

We do this on a conscious level. It is a decision that we all make at some point in our lives. However, few of us realize that we also do this on a subconscious level. Even a professional who we know nothing about, we give more weight to their opinion and place it higher than any others. It is because it is our way of acknowledging their experience, position, and knowledge.

It is interesting to note that this automatic acceptance can be seen not just in numbers but also in social settings all around the world. Doctors are able to get their patients to follow certain regimens of treatment if their diplomas are openly displayed in their offices when they make recommendations. People are more likely to obey traffic laws if there is a uniformed officer present, and most are inclined to listen to an expert on any subject if there is some indication that he is indeed an expert.

Of course, this strategy can also backfire on you. If you were to go around boasting about your accomplishments or you were to tell everyone that they have to listen to you because you're the expert, it can be off-putting to many people and shut them down. However, if someone else was to point to your level of experience in a particular area and recommend you, people are more inclined to respond favorably.

This is why you see countless testimonials on webpages that want to sell you something. Interestingly enough, you don't need to know the trustworthiness of the person who is making the recommendations. In most cases, just the suggestion from an outside person is enough to convince people of the weight of the authority is all that is needed. Studies that have shown that this type of referral strategy can yield an increase of as much as 20% results in many cases.

**Consistency:** People generally will always follow the same path they have traveled in the past. They defer to something familiar and comfortable. Therefore, if someone naturally has done something for you in the past, it is quite likely that they will do it again; in most cases, their next action will even be bigger than before.

If you can get someone to make a small and insignificant commitment the first time, then it is likely that they will make an even larger gesture later on. Businesses tap into this natural desire by asking first for small but voluntary commitments like filling out an online form or answering a simple survey question. In one such health center, patients were asked to fill out their own appointment card rather than the staff. As a result, they had an 18% drop in missed appointments. But the act was so miniscule and minor the patient never even realized they were actually making a commitment.

**Liking:** We all naturally gravitate to the people and things we like. This is because of three essential elements. First, we want to be with those who are similar to us and we can relate to. Second, we are attracted to those who compliment us, and third those people who are willing to work with us and help us to achieve our goals.

Many have become successful by finding ways to point out similarities between their goals and their potential customers. By taking the time to engage in some form of small talk, sharing personal information with each other, you create a bond that will bind the two of you together on some level. The stronger you can make that bond before you begin to make a request, the better chance that the person will be willing to grant your request. Businesses that have used this strategy have seen as much as a 90% positive response as opposed to those who had a 55% response when they just got right down to business.

To use this skill to your advantage, look for common ground that you might share with others and give them genuine compliments rather than canned platitudes, and you should see better results.

**Consensus:** Consensus is the gentle use of peer pressure. People tend to follow the crowd in their actions and beliefs, especially if they are not sure of themselves. All of us take notice of what other people are doing. We often choose a restaurant because of how busy it is. We assume that if it is always busy it must be good. McDonald's displays the number of customers they've served over the many years they have been in business and you've probably already noticed how Amazon has a list of other products customers are buying when they choose anything you've searched for.

It's all part of our culture of socialization. Applying this to our art of persuasion gives people a sense of camaraderie with us and helps people to connect to not just what we have to offer but also to others who have already become a part of who we are. Whether you're selling a product or you're just trying to get someone to agree with you, one of the simplest ways to get people on board is to let them know that if they join you, they will not be alone. It feels less risky when they know they have someone to join forces with.

Any one of these strategies can help you to achieve better results when you're looking to get certain things. You've probably already begun to realize how many times you've been manipulated in your everyday life. No doubt, you believed you were making your own decision, which is probably true to a certain extent, but there's no question that the idea that germinated in your mind was planted there by someone else.

## How to Use Persuasive Body Language

One thing that few people realize is that when you communicate with others, it is not the words that most people connect with. The foundation of your communication style lies not on what comes off your lips but on what your body is doing. Careful attention must be given to how you present your message. A poorly delivered speech can do so much more damage than a poorly developed presentation. To get the most of your message, your aim should be to tap into their subconscious mind on a more physical level. Here are just a few of the most commonly used body language signals. As you read through them visualize them in your head, practice them in a small scale when with others and watch how easily you can bring people into your fold.

## Be Superman

The Superman pose works because it makes you stand out from the rest. Practice this in the privacy of your home before going out. Slip into the bathroom and try standing erect, puff out your chest (not too much), and place your hands on your hips with your elbows pointing out to the sides. Your goal is to make yourself look as big as possible. Do this pose before you begin your presentation and notice how your confidence and poise begins to grow.

## Stand Up Tall

It can be pretty easy to slip into a slouch but fight the urge. It's important for you to stand tall so you project the best possible image you can. When you speak publicly with your body erect, your shoulders pulled back, and your body straight you'll not only look more confident but you'll feel it too. However, there is another benefit to standing tall that is not so readily seen. When you stand up tall, you align your airway so that your breath flows in and out freely. With all the potential blockages open, you'll naturally speak louder, your voice will be cleaner, and you'll sound as well as appear more professional.

**Keep Your Body Open**

You do need to be careful with the standing tall pose. You can overdo it and instead of displaying poise and confidence you could come off as being cocky and arrogant. To avoid this, resist any temptation to cross your arms as that will make you appear closed off. Try not to stuff your hands in your pocket, and if you are sitting don't cross your legs. You want to appear confident but also trustworthy so the more open you can keep your limbs the more people will want to respond to your message.

**Make Eye Contact**

If you want to give your presentation a more personal touch, work hard at making true eye contact. When you look directly into someone's eyes, you are basically inviting them into your inner fold. Direct eye contact creates an unspoken bond that feels more receptive than just talking at a person.

Of course, you don't want to stare into their eyes because that might make them feel a little uncomfortable. So, make eye contact with them, but only hold it for a few seconds. If you're speaking to a group of people, pick out several people in the crowd and make eye contact with each of them. After a few seconds move to the next person and continue this with as many people as is reasonably possible. It makes listeners feel that you're giving them a personal touch and that you are genuinely interested in them.

**Move Around**

If you're giving a presentation, resist the temptation to stand there like a statue. Whenever possible walkaround and use as much space as you can. It will reflect a more natural movement and give you more confidence. If you are nervous, movement will help you to relax in the environment and get your message across more easily. Movement also makes it possible for you to project your voice into different areas of the room so more people can connect with your message.

**Use Your Hands**

Remember, let your whole body talk. Communication involves more than words. Keep your hands free so that you can gesture freely. This will draw more people from your audience to you. Let your hands move freely to emphasize the points you want to make. Common gestures you can include could be pointing to your palm to stress a specific point, palms open wide and spread out to the sides to indicate openness or to create a question in the audience's mind and pointing outwards to stress other matters.

It would help a great deal if you were to take some time and observe how you communicate naturally with people you know. Very few people speak comfortably without gestures, you just don't realize you're doing it. However, if you start to take note of how your hands and body move when you speak with friends, you'll know which gestures you can incorporate into any presentation you make to give it the extra push to take your message over the top.

**Use Facial Expressions**

We say a lot with our face and when people speak to you, they will subconsciously look for those cues to fill in the blanks of what you didn't or can't say verbally. When they ask you a very basic question like, "how are you?" they immediately watch your face when you give the answer. Our faces are like blank canvases and when we speak our message is reflected on it projecting our inner feelings. Without saying a word, a person can tell how we are feeling, what we are thinking, and whether or not they want to trust you.

When you make facial gestures, keep your face relaxed. A calm and relaxed face can give you the appearance of authenticity and make you feel more human.

Keep these facial gestures to a minimum. Too many and people will feel uncomfortable – too little and people will think you are uninterested.

Becoming a master manipulator is just a matter of perfecting an art that we have been learning since childhood. It is not something new, unique, or questionable. It is just refining our way of communicating with the outside world. What we've just discussed in this first chapter are the basics of this skill. Now, let's roll up our sleeves and look a little deeper under the surface to see what really drives people to follow a true master in the art of persuasion.

# Chapter 2: Emotional Intelligence 101

For years, the common belief was that the key to success lies in your Intelligence quotient or your IQ. Whether you are book smart or street smart, there is no question that having some level of mental acuity will help you navigate the obstacles that you must overcome to achieve your goals.

But that leads us into a long-standing debate, which one is more important? Those who advocate for IQ as the most important argue that your mental intelligence is what will help you to navigate the system will definitely pave the way for you but evidence is now emerging that shows that emotional intelligence is equally as important in preparing you to deal with people. To clarify this though, we need to fully understand the difference between the two.

Well known psychologist, Howard Gardner points out that one's intelligence is not limited to mastering one single ability. His years of study in how the brain works has identified several different ways one can show intelligence. Read any of his writings and you'll come across his well-known expression:

***It's not how smart you are but how you are smart***

Where IQ focuses on one or a few abilities, commonly referred to as the "G Factor," he points out that the ability to recognize emotions, understand, and express them clearly is key to how well one may be able to navigate the challenges in life.

If you've ever taken an IQ test then you know that it only focuses on certain skills. Your IQ score was based only on visual, spatial, working memory, short and long-term memory, quantitative and fluid reasoning. In essence, you were tested on the general topics commonly taught in school.

Your EQ, however, is measured on your ability to perceive an emotion, evaluate, manage, and express it. When you have emotional intelligence, you are able to see and identify the emotions in others, reason on your observations to determine how others are feeling and use those emotions as a means of facilitating communication all while keeping your own emotions in check.

For years, we've always placed great store in our IQ and it is still viewed as important even today. However, as our knowledge of how the brain works continues to grow, there is increasing evidence that the IQ alone is not a guarantee of success. It's true, people with a high IQ will usually do better in school, they get the better jobs, and even seem to be more physically healthy. But throughout history, we have repeatedly seen many with high IQs that seem to fail at everything they attempt. It is clear that IQ alone will not get you to where you want to be. Rather it is an entire battery of factors that include your EQ that will give you better assurance at success.

## What Is Emotional Intelligence?

We've already determined that at the heart of it, emotional intelligence is the ability to identify and recognize emotions in others and manage your own, but there is more to it than that. In order to have good emotional intelligence, you need to master three skills.

- **Emotional Awareness:** The ability to recognize emotions in others and label them. It's not enough to say that person is upset, you need to know whether they are angry, sad, frightened, grieving, or embarrassed.
- **Redirect:** Once you've identified those emotions, you need to skillfully redirect those emotions by thinking things through,

use them to solve problems, and apply them to the tasks or skills you need to meet.
- **Manage:** The skill in managing your own emotions goes beyond just not throwing a fit when you don't like something. As long as you can manage those feelings and use them to your advantage, you will become a master of emotional intelligence.

When you have a high EQ, you are able to identify a wide range of both negative and positive emotions, even when they are not obviously displayed. You will be in-tune with how other people are feeling, which can give you insight into what they are thinking, and you'll be able to pick up on even the subtlest of cues when you are interacting within a particular social environment. All of these skills can be used to help you become a better spouse, friend, parent, teacher, lover, leader, boss, or anything else you might wish to do.

It would be difficult to get someone to respond to you if you don't know what moves them to take action. There is a delicate art to managing emotions, but it is necessary for anyone who is looking to expand their horizons.

Emotions are extremely powerful and are the force behind all of our behavior and by extension the behavior of all people, triggering both positive and negative reactions. Your EQ will help you to focus on not just your own personal feelings and thoughts, but also on those of others.

If you take the time, you could probably look back and find plenty of examples of how others have used their EQ to manipulate you in the past. The tactic was subtle, you likely had no idea it was happening. For example, how many times have you been watching TV and saw a commercial showing young children from a third world country with distended bellies and flies and mosquitos buzzing around them. It pulls on your heart strings, doesn't it? Or perhaps you met up with a friend who was visibly distressed and after some prodding, told you how he was in a bad financial state and needed some help to pay off some financial obligations.

In each of those cases, the manipulator pulled on your emotional heartstrings because they knew how it would affect you emotionally. They were able to get you in a position to want to help them. In fact, you probably thought that it was your idea all along. Every day, we see these kinds of emotional manipulators all around us, most of them are used in a positive and beneficial way, but there are plenty examples of negatives ones as well.

Consider one example of one manipulation master that caused extreme harm to others. Before Adolf Hitler began his reign of terror as the head of the Nazi regime, he spent years observing human behavior and how his own body language was affecting those around him. He observed the emotional impact of every gesture and position and honed those skills until he turned himself into a mesmerizing speaker.

A leader who wants to take unfair advantage over others will use many things to get them to buy into a specific idea.
They may try to control you by using your own fears against you, even going to the point of exaggerating the truth or telling you outright lies to back you into a corner where you feel they are the only ones you can trust.

They could also resort to outright deception to put you at a disadvantage. They may tell you the truth but only part of the story; the part that shows them in a more positive light. They will say all the things you want to hear. So, they may be the yes person in the office, always agreeing with you on every point, regardless of the logic. They will do you small favors in an attempt to get you to be indebted to them. They will try everything they can to maneuver things to their advantage. This strategy puts you in a setting where they have the power and you are not as at ease as you would be otherwise. Meetings will be at their home, office, club, or any other location of their choosing.

They are not afraid to ask the hard questions. This is an attempt to uncover your weaknesses or to gather information they could one day use to manipulate you further. Often the questions are about personal matters or things you are less likely to discuss openly.

They talk fast to try to throw you off track and may even use uncommon vocabulary in order to undermine your confidence. Think of those fast talking infomercials you see on late-night TV. They usually throw extensive vocabulary at you in the hopes that you won't be able to follow their storyline fully. And the rapid-paced speech doesn't give you enough time to process all the information they are giving you, leaving you unsure of yourself.

They are not afraid of showing their emotions or causing a scene when it will work to their advantage. Negative situations often make people uncomfortable which can give them a huge advantage that they can exploit.

They will pressure you to respond to situations quickly so you don't have time to think about it. They want you to react on impulse even to what may seem like unreasonable demands.

They may even cut off communication altogether in order to unnerve you and give them the upper hand. This gives them a sense of power and forces you to wait until they are ready to continue the relationship.

All of these are tactics that negative manipulators use at will. As you read through them, there is a good chance that you have seen these used on you from time to time. In fact, you may have even used them yourself on other people.

As a master manipulator, it is important that you recognize these tactics. None of these would work if you recognized them firsthand, and if you had a high enough EQ, you would know how to respond in order to avoid being manipulated in ways that you're not comfortable with.

If they try to use fear – take the time to examine the bigger picture, gather more information so you would have all the facts to make a decision.

If they are being deceptive – ask questions to uncover the truth or speak to someone trustworthy to verify the facts of the situation.

If they are being too agreeable – focus on having a more balanced thinking process.
If they are always doing you small favors – don't hesitate to say no and refuse them.

If they always want to control location – insist on a neutral meeting place.

If they ask too many personal questions – avoid saying too much.

If they speak too fast – stop them to ask questions for verification.

If they are prone to emotional outbursts – avoid impulse reactions. Wait for them to calm down and speak to them in a slow and purposeful manner to balance the situation.

If they are pressuring you to make a decision quickly – request more time or refuse.

If they are giving you the silent treatment – be willing to walk away or at least wait until they come to you, giving you the advantage.

Another masterful manipulator of the 20th century was Martin Luther King, Jr. Take some time and read over his *I Have A Dream* speech and ask yourself why it was so powerful. Why decades later, the words continue to resonate with everyone who reads or hears them. It was his choice of words, meant to stir up and touch on the emotions of his listeners. At the same time, as he delivered his message, he was able to keep complete control of his own emotions, letting out only what was needed to stir the audience to align with him.

So, while your IQ may be instrumental in positioning you in the right place to achieve some level of success, it is your EQ that will be most effective in getting others to go along with your grand plan so you can get the results you seek. No doubt, you'll need both, but your EQ will be the bigger indication of success.

## Why Master Manipulators Need Emotional Intelligence

Lisa Nowak was a highly intelligent person. By the time she had applied for her job at NASA, she had met all the qualifications. She had completed a Master's program in aeronautical engineering and a postgraduate study in astrophysics at the US Naval Academy. She had spent more than five years accumulating five years of piloting experience. She was physically fit and had all the book knowledge she could have possibly need. She was selected to be in the astronaut program with no problems.

Unfortunately, things didn't work out well for Lisa. In 2007, her inability to control her emotions caused her to make a rash decision that destroyed her chances completely. When she discovered that her then romantic partner was involved with someone else, she took matters into her own hands. She took the 15 hour drive from Houston to Orlando to confront and kidnap the other woman, which lead to her having an emotional breakdown, going to jail ending her career completely.

The evidence is clear, one's EQ dictates how we behave. Our behavior is the end result of a linear process that is played out in our brains.

1. A triggering event occurs
2. Our senses pick up the event and transmits it to our brain
3. We mentally process the event and produce thoughts and opinions about it
4. The thoughts trigger an emotional response
5. The emotion we feel triggers a specific behavior
6. The behavior then triggers another inciting event
7. The cycle starts all over again

The key to becoming a master manipulator is to control behavior and since all behavior is triggered by our emotional state, it is important to manage emotions well. No matter what we do with others, communication, relationships, business, or anything else, the emotions are behind the entire process. If you have a high EQ it will be easier for you to read other people and manipulate situations in order to get them to do what you expect.

Most of us can identify and recognize our own emotions and how they cause us to react to triggering events in our lives. However, where we often find ourselves lacking is in the ability to see those same reactions in others. One of the most important factors in mastering a high EQ is to identify emotional reactions in others.

According to one study conducted by Johnson & Johnson, higher performers in the workplace were those who showed a higher emotional intelligence. The numbers were quite impressive showing 90% of the best workers were those with a high EQ and 80% of the lowest showed a low EQ.

No matter what your goals are or how you plan to use your manipulation skills, a high EQ can be one of the most significant factors in getting you to where you want to be.

9 Ways to Develop Powerful Emotional Intelligence

Because emotions are so powerful, they have a direct effect on how well you interact in social situations. They can also dictate your coping strategies, the amount of money you spend, and what you do with your time. As you can see controlling your emotions could be one of the most important factors in determining your success no matter what you do.

Keep in mind that there is a big difference between developing emotional intelligence and suppressing your emotions. If you feel sad or you try to hide your feelings, it could cause you more harm than good. Suppressing emotions are generally what leads to damaging coping skills like over-eating, gambling, and drinking.

Managing your emotions and developing a high EQ is not hiding or suppressing your feelings but is recognizing those feelings and not allowing them to have the power to control you. In other words, you control your emotions not the other way around. So, if you find yourself in a bad mood, you need to take the helm and change it by choosing to display another emotion. But learning how to manage them will take an investment in time and practice. Here are a few skills that will help you get started on the right path.

**1. Identify Negative Emotions First**

Generally, the emotions that are most likely to get us into trouble are the negative ones. When our negative emotions take control, we often make impulse reactions. We need to take the time to analyze what is going on inside our heads. By taking the time to stop and think about what's happening internally before you become overly emotional, you are less likely to have a knee-jerk reaction to a triggering event. Learn to breathe a little and try to look at things more objectively. Practicing the art of mindfulness can help you to slow down and analyze a situation objectively from different perspectives. Once you have identified your emotion and labeled it, you cross a mental threshold that makes it easier to move forward.

**2. Change Your Vocabulary**

Your choice of words you use to communicate says a lot about who you are inside. Analyze your language to see which words you're using to relay what you want. Those with a higher level of emotional intelligence are very specific when they speak while those with a low EQ tend to be very vague, sounding like they are skirting issues rather than addressing them. The next time you're in a conversation with someone else that didn't go well, take the time to analyze the words you used. How could you have been clearer in your communication. Chances are you will start to see your own communication deficiencies, but also recognize emotional triggers in others. This will give you a better chance of addressing the problem rather than allowing your emotions to catapult you into a cycle of negative behavior.

### 3. Learn to be More Empathetic

Start watching other people more closely. People subconsciously give you both verbal and non-verbal cues letting you know what emotions they are feeling. This can give you invaluable insight into what actions you need to take or words you need to say to change the dynamic. Before you react though, take the time to put yourself in their place and ask yourself how you would want someone to react. This can be a key communication tool that can lead to better connections with others and remind yourself that every situation is not always about you.

### 4. Learn Your Stressors

All of us have our own triggers, events that cause us stress and anxiety. These stressors are what can take you out of the game so, if you know what they are, you can develop strategies that can address them before you react negatively. So, if you know that looking at the bills gets your blood boiling, put it off to a time when you are less likely to have to interact with other people. If you know that the phone ringing during dinner time causes you to get angry, unplug the phone until dinner is over. By being proactive in these situations, you can avoid negative altercations with others.

### 5. Don't Allow Challenges to Bring You Down

No matter who you are, we all are faced with challenges. That in itself is not an indicator of the kind of person you are. It's the behavior that those challenges trigger that can tell the world who you are. How you address uncomfortable issues can either put you on the path to success or bring you down. So, when faced with unpleasant situations, learn how to take a more optimistic view rather than a critical one. For example, if you find you are having difficulties with your employer, you can either leave the office constantly complaining about what he or she said, or you can ask yourself constructive questions and try to come up with proactive strategies to diffuse the situation. Learn how to address the conflict before it arises and take on a more optimistic approach. This will gradually start to change your personal behavior and will start to draw more people to you.

### 6. Strive to Understand the Reason Behind Your Emotions

Once you have been able to identify which emotions you are experiencing, you need to try to understand why. Your goal is to discover the triggering event that caused these emotions to form. It may take a little time, but rarely is the triggering event the true cause of the feelings. You may find that you have to look further back in your life to find out why certain events cause you to react the way you do. Quite often it is not the event that causes your distress but the fact that the situation does not honor your personal values in some way. This will require you to develop some cold hard honesty to help you uncover your own hidden truths.

### 7. Resolve the Issue

Sometimes all that is needed to diffuse a difficult situation is to learn how to look at it from a different perspective. Remember the cycle – thoughts lead to emotions which lead to behavior. If you are feeling bad about something, go back to your thoughts to change the dialogue. After you've identified the triggering thought, try to think of different possible thoughts that can change the outcome. Focus on the positive and the negative feelings usually will go away. Other times, you might find that much of the negativity you've built up can be alleviated simply by understanding what's happening. This redirect process is key to gaining command over your emotions and usually leads to a much calmer personality.

### 8. Make a Different Choice

After you've resolved the issue in your mind, you need to make the decision to react a different way in the future. This can be quite difficult, because we know that in the heat of the moment, rational thinking is never truly the case. But a lot of our behavior is actually the result of habits; we have automatically behaviors with certain situations and we have done so for so long that we don't even stop to consider if our response is working or not. No one wants to be the guy that flies off the handle at the slightest provocation; it's stressful on everyone including him. Make a choice today, to not allow your emotions to hijack you and lead you down the path towards destruction. Learning to master this skill is not something you can just read about and the next day you know exactly what to do. You will fail many times, you will struggle with restraining yourself, but you will gradually make a change.

### 9. Minimize Negative Moods

When you do find yourself in a bad mood, readjust as soon as possible, otherwise you could find yourself engaging in behavior that will isolate you. Avoid being evasive, this can actually work against your attempts to become a master manipulator. You might find yourself complaining about the people around you or slip into a scenario of not talking or lashing out at others.

So, it is smart to plan ahead. Think of the things that generally put you in a better mood so you can start doing those things when negative feelings start to rise up. For example, you might want to talk about pleasant things with a friend, listen to your favorite music, take a walk, or meditate. It will keep your mind focused on what's important so that you can get away from the negative feelings before they become a problem.

It is one thing to identify emotions and understand them but managing them can be very difficult. Our emotions are not constant and can rise and fall like the waves of the sea so it can be hard to keep them under control. No one is pleasant all the time and no one is always a hot head. We all have certain triggers that bring out the ugly in us, but if you practice these steps often enough, eventually you will begin to see the tide changing and you'll get the mastery over them. As you do, your EQ will become stronger and you'll be more in-tuned with your own inner demons. This will give you the needed confidence to handle uncomfortable situations by shifting your mood and give you more control over any situation you find yourself in.

## How to Control Your Emotions Like a Boss

When you feel like the world is closing in on you, there is a powerful but overwhelming sense that you are losing control, which can be a very frightening thing. It doesn't matter if it deals with something at home or in the boardroom with a team of professionals. The pressure from a constant stream of things piling up can make you feel claustrophobic causing you to do something quickly to change it. It can be these times that cause us to make our biggest impulse reactions, which are usually the ones to get us into trouble.

At times, taking a few deep breaths or a walk around the block just doesn't cut it. As the cortisone in your body starts to increase, you feel your chest tighten or the knot in your stomach starts to grow. You start to yell and scream at anyone within your vicinity, whether they are responsible or not. You may threaten, or you could storm out of the room, slamming the door behind you in a child-like tantrum. That is the moment when you are on the verge of exploding. How can you reclaim your life and make sure that your emotions stay in check even when everything seems out of your hands.

We've all had that scenario or something similar happen to us. Later we are riddled with guilt and shame for our behavior. But what we may not realize is that your emotions have triggered a chemical reaction in your body, which started a snowball effect that once started was almost impossible to control.

On the other hand, we have all seen that one boss, parent, teacher, or other authority figure that seems to maintain their composure no matter how desperate the situation may seem. What's the difference? It comes down to one simple factor. They were able to control their emotions so that the negative behavior never starts in the first place. The truth is that managing your emotions can literally transform your life and personality, enabling you to bring out the best qualities within you rather than the worst.

If you can relate to either of these situations, it should become clear to you that emotions are not inherently bad. We all have them for a reason; they are there to warn us of situations that are uncomfortable, dangerous, or unpleasant. But, since schools are primarily focused on teaching us book knowledge, most of us have to learn to manage our emotions on our own and we never outgrow those temper tantrum habits we displayed as a child.

It doesn't have to be this way though. By making a concerted effort to take charge of your emotions, you can literally begin to take charge of the situation. Rather than allowing your own emotions to direct your behavior, you direct your emotions. How can you do this?

By developing something called emotion regulation skills. In essence, these are unique skills designed to manage those impulse urges and emotions that rise up in all of us. The more you master these skills the more confidence you'll have in managing your emotions and controlling them. This will be a major step in your training to become a master manipulator. It's a X step process:

## 1. Identify your feelings and accept them for what they are

You can't manage what you can't understand. But it is not enough to say, "I'm angry" or "I'm frustrated." This is a starting point but aim to be more specific in your identifying process. Are you angry because you're afraid? Are you frustrated because of the workload or because you feel unqualified to manage it? By identifying the root cause of the negative emotion, you begin to understand what your true emotions are. Rarely, are the ones we reveal to the public a true image of who we are.

It is important that you get rid of the need to judge yourself. Your goal here is to merely identify the situation, not justify, explain, or judge. Acknowledge it for what it is, don't resist them, just accept them for what they are and move on. You'll address the correction of these habits later on.

It is important to do this as soon as you notice an emotional surge begin to rise. Work at expanding your vocabulary and go beyond just stating the obvious. As you work on developing these skills, you will soon be able to discern even the slightest changes in your mood swings.

a. Identify that you are having an emotion
b. Pause and analyze
c. What thoughts are running through your mind
d. What sensations are you feeling in your body
e. Identify the emotion
f. Try to discern the nuances and what changed
g. What is the reaction you are trying to suppress
h. Observe

Here, you are working as an outside observer. Rather than allowing the emotion to unfold within you, use your imagination and allow it to play out in front of you as if it was an actor on a stage. Let happen, watch it intensify and then dissipate without making yourself a part of it.

**2. Take Positive Action**

Once you are familiar with the emotion, you will find it much easier to manage it. As you observe the emotion playing out in front of you, pull back the curtain to see the bigger picture. In most cases, you will be able to bring your mind to a calmer state. Often just taking the time to identify and look at the bigger scope is enough to bring you into a more stable frame of mind.

If that doesn't work, you can take the next step and find something that can distract you from your negative feelings at the time. Try to have a calming task you can do on hand to bring your mind back into balance. Many people turn to something they instinctively enjoy like walking, journaling, deep breathing, crafting, or coloring. The key here is to have something that will naturally relax you. All of us are different so your calming activity may be something unique to everyone around you.

By mastering your emotion regulation, you will naturally become more confident and empowered. Once your emotions are no longer controlling you, it will be easier for you to see how you can master manipulation. The bottom line is that you can never hope to manipulate others until you are able to manipulate yourself. Once you have developed your EQ well, you will not only see how it changes you internally, but by extension have a positive effect on everyone around you. It will take dedication and hard work. You won't be able to accomplish it right away and it will take a lot of practice, but the results will pay off for you many times over and you will be able to see the advantages in the changes as you progress.

# Chapter Three: Choosing Your Target

After going through the process outlined in the last chapter, chances are you've come to learn something new about yourself. Most people are surprised to learn what really makes them tick, and it's even more surprising to discover what their triggers actually are. Now that you understand yourself better, it is easier to determine exactly what you need to change your circumstances and move towards your goal. You can't manipulate or influence other people, if you can't manipulate yourself.

Another advantage of mastering the skills in the last chapter is that you become more aware of others around you. By paying more attention to both verbal and non-verbal cues they give, you will almost feel like you're a mind reader. You will be able to discern their moods, wants, fears, desires, etc. This knowledge can be used to find your first target for manipulation.

When choosing a target, look for certain traits that the individual demonstrates to show they are open to receiving and responding to your powers of influence. So, as you scope out potential prospects, look for these characteristics. Don't assume that if someone is displaying these qualities that they are in some way inferior to you or others. To the contrary, many of the following qualities are quite admirable. As we've already stated, any facet of a person's character can be used in both a positive and a negative way. We are only looking for a doorway to enter and implement a possible means of exercising your powers of persuasion.

**They are Conscientious**

People who are conscientious are not likely to be focusing entirely on themselves. Conscientious people are concerned about the quality of their work, the welfare of others, and their commitment to any task that has been assigned to them. While they may be concerned about how events will affect them, their primary concern will be determined by their moral compass. In order to exercise some level of influence over them, you need to tap into their powerful sense of morality. Once you can show them how they can achieve their goals in relation to that, you will have a powerful means in which to persuade them to do what you want them to do.

**They Have Empathy**

A good target will have strong empathetic tendencies. Empathy can be viewed as the emotional fuel that you can use to propel you towards your goals. People with empathy often are given praise, attention and valuable resources freely, putting you in a state of comfort as you make your requests or needs know.

Empathetic people are excellent at putting themselves in your shoes. They can feel your pain in their heart and because of this, they will do everything within their power to relieve you of it. You can use that empathy to your advantage by telling a store, apologizing, or carefully framing a scenario to gain their sympathy.

**They Have Integrity**

A person with integrity is true to their word and can be of immense value to you. They are not inclined to cheat or steal, nor are they likely to break off a relationship until it is absolutely necessary. Even if they realize later that you have taken unfair advantage of them, their sense of integrity is usually what keeps them from retaliation. The relationship you build with them will be strong and their entire sense of being will keep them from betraying it no matter what.

**They are Resilient**

A good target will be resilient enough to bounce back from any incidents that may cause them harm. This resiliency makes them strong enough to stand up against of the pressures you can put on them. Even if they are faced with difficult challenges these are the people who are less likely to give up. While all their instincts may be telling them to run the other way, they are more likely to stay the course in spite of it all.

Establishing a relationship with them is the same as obligating them to you. They are unlikely to turn on you even if they discover that they are being manipulated.

**They are Sentimental**

A person who is very sentimental leads with his heart in everything he does. A manipulator can use flattery and praise to position the target and set them up for persuasion. The words used need to address their unique needs and desires. By idolizing them from the very start of the relationship, you can garner their trust and appeal to their most basic need for love. Creating pleasant memories together pulls at their heartstrings and bonds them into a relationship you can use later to get what you want.

They best way to influence a sentimentalist is to carefully study them, determine their individual qualities and the things that they value the most. By establishing a relationship with them and picking up on their verbal-and non-verbal cues, you can uncover their insecurities and weaknesses.

These are the basic characteristics you will find in those who are easy targets for manipulation. It doesn't mean that they are the only one you will be able to work your magic with, but these are the ones you will most likely find success with as you start to apply the manipulation strategies will we be discussing throughout this book.

What Hooks People In?

Anything that draws our attention can be used as a key tool of manipulation. So, when choosing a target to persuade in one way or another, it is important that you use those things that will naturally hook people and draw them into you. Your hook, however, needs to be something that your target won't have to think too much about. In fact, you don't even want them to get even the slightest inkling that you're pulling them in. With the right skill, you will be able to subtly draw them into your circle without ever making them consciously aware that they are caught in your web.

Whether you're trying to entice a love interest or you're trying to get your foot in the door of your next job, your first task is to draw the person in. This can be tricky and the answers can vary depending on your target. However, there are common threads you can find in all sorts of people. Since most people are more inclined to listen to you when they feel respected it's a given that if you can tap into their personal sense of self, you'll be halfway there. Consider these very basic qualities and test them out to see if they will work with your intended target.

**Become a Good Listener**: People will naturally be drawn to you if they feel that you are listening to what they have to say. But this involves more than just giving the appearance that you are interested in what they have to say. When you are a dedicated listener, you are fully engaged in their message.

This does several things that can work in your favor. First, you'll become a better communicator but you will also be building up a level of trust between you and the other person. That rapport will work on a subconscious level slowly building up a deeper and more meaningful connection between the two of you.

An active listener requires commitment and focus. It may not be easy at first, but to show keen interest in what the other person is saying. That means not responding to distractions or interruptions but being completely present in the moment. You may have to ask questions for clarification, regularly insert words in the conversation so they know you're still with them, turning off or not answering your phone when calls come in, and giving your whole attention to them.

**Being Observant**

Active listening also means watching the other person's non-verbal cues as well. You will be paying close attention to their body language and verbal intonation. In other words, you want to not only hear what they are saying to you but how they are saying it. This will give you valuable information about their emotional state of mind.

For example, if they are whimpering or speaking in a low tone of voice it may be a sign that they are worried or fearful. However, if they are shouting it could be an indication that they are angry or frustrated.

But in order for these observations to draw them in, you need to find ways to show them that you are committed to them. By mirroring back some of their expressions, and clarifying your understanding of those points, you are demonstrating to them that you are kindling a new relationship with them. It will endear them to you on a subconscious level. The more they are able to believe that you value their input and their message, the more attractive you will be to them and they will respond to you accordingly.

**Kindness**

We live in a world where true and genuine kindness is hard to find. If you want to really hook people in, just a simple act of kindness may be all that is needed. Kindness does not necessarily mean the giving of gifts. While that may be a part of it, sometimes just the habit of saying kind words, smiling, or showing a genuine active of consideration may be all that is needed to show people that you care.

This should not come as a surprise to you. You've probably already experienced how you respond to people who are kind to you. You should think no less of those who you are trying to lure into your circle. In fact, it has been scientifically proven that both men and women are more drawn to people who are compassionate and selfless. It is actually quite a powerful means of attracting others and can literally influence a person even if the kindness is not shown to them. In other words, it can also work if they are just mere observers of your acts of kindness even if they are not the recipient.

The concept of kindness can be extended beyond the obvious. A 2013 study showed that both men and women were drawn to people who had a more helping spirit, actually finding them to be more attractive on all levels. Demonstrating a preference for others in a helpful manner can appeal to people on the most basic of levels as this is an indication that a helpful person will fill need for protection in a dangerous world.

**Smiling**

Hooking people can be as easy as smiling. It is the one act that will cost you nothing but can yield you lots of results. Smiling not only makes you stand out as kind and helpful, but it also releases your own endorphins and serotonin in your body. Both of these naturally produced chemicals will not only improve your own mood but is infectious enough to improve the mood of those around you, including your target.

Studies have shown that just seeing a smiling face can activate the pleasure center of the brain giving your target a sense of satisfaction and reward. According to the School of Psychology conducted at the University of Aberdeen in Scotland, those who received smiles from others (even if indirectly) were naturally drawn to the smiler.

**Consistency**

People crave stability in their lives. If you're serious about drawing other people to you then consistency is the key. Instability in jobs, home life, even our diets cause people distress. Life becomes unpredictable and confusing. A person who has an inconsistent person in their lives never gain the ability to feel secure.

Your target will naturally be drawn to you on a subconscious level if your behavior is consistent and reliable. To reinforce this gravitational pull, if your consistency is in line with their personal attitudes, beliefs, and core values it will be that much easier to draw them in.

**Obligation**

People can also be hooked and drawn over to you by obligating them to you. This is interesting in that quite often the obligation starts even before you do anything directly. Think of the company that offers a free gift of very little value. Sometimes referred to as the theory of reciprocity, it is a concept that is deeply ingrained in us from a very early age. When someone does something for us, we feel indebted to reciprocate in some way. They may not expect anything in return, but the power is so strong that it compels us anyway.

This power is so strong that there is only one way to rid ourselves of this need to return like for like is to do something for the other person. Even if you don't want or even like the gift or favor, you feel compelled to follow through quite often with a sense of urgency. It is a kind of psychological debt that can sometimes be so strong that it drives a person to sometimes exceed the original gift many times over.

**Connection**

It's a natural inclination in all of us. The more connected we are to others the more influence they have over our decisions. By creating a bond, you create comfort in others. Even if you've known them only a short time that bond can make it seem like a lifelong relationship.

There are four main elements to a strong connection:

- Attraction: By choosing a single positive quality and using it to influence the general perception, people will naturally feel connected to you. By displaying qualities like kindness, intelligence, and loyalty, people will find you more attractive.

- Rapport: Rapport is a little bit more difficult to define. It is a hidden quality that puts you on the same mental wavelength as the other person. It's that feeling you get when you meet someone and instantly hit it off. That secret something that automatically bonds you to another person. Sometimes rapport is readily recognizable as in a physical attraction or a common understanding. Other times it is a little harder to identify. You've probably seen cases where two people have no obvious common ground but they develop a rapport just the same.

- People skills (EQ): Your ability to work well with people can forge a strong bond with them. According to some research, at least 85% of your success will depend on how you interact with others; the other 15% can be related to your intelligence and specific training. As we discussed in the last chapter, your EQ is crucial to your ability to take that knowledge and skill base and connect it to other people.

- Similarity: People are naturally drawn to things they are familiar with. So, by utilizing those characteristics that people feel comfortable with, you can connect to more people. Studies have revealed that people are naturally attracted to things they can relate to and understand. By matching your personality traits with their lifestyles, they will be impelled to connect to you.

When all four of these elements are in play you can build a strong bond that long-standing relationships can be founded upon.

**Social Pressure**

Because we are social creatures by nature, all of us, no matter how shy, have an inborn desire to belong to something. A good manipulator will definitely look for someone who is searching for some form of inclusion to his advantage. For all of us, if the desire to become a group is strong enough, it can easily cause us to change our viewpoint and perceptions just so we can fit in.

We all care to some extent, about what others think of us and we all seek validation, even if we don't want to admit it. It is this inborn desire to fit in with the main crowd that determines our view of what is considered "correct" behavior. If our actions go against the mainstream of the masses, our behavior is frowned upon, but the more we fit in, the "correct" others will perceive us and the more likely they will be willing to conform to what you want. It is a natural part of human nature, and the more you can create an approved form of social pressure, the more your targets will feel validated and bond with you.

**Scarcity**

People have an inner drive to not miss out on things. This is why limited time offers usually work very well when it comes to sales. The natural tendency is to put things off until a later time when there is no real immediate need, but by creating sense of urgency, you can trigger an impulse reaction that will compel people to move even if their own minds tell them it's not necessary.

Scarcity triggers that inborn fear of missing out or FOMO. Think of how things work in an auction. Usually at an auction, there is a limited supply of a specific item (often only one). When another person outbids you, a sort of panic starts to set in. What if you can't find this item again, what if someone considers the item more valuable than you? Perhaps you missed something? All sorts of thoughts start to running through your head and suddenly, the drive to obtain that item becomes more powerful than your own common sense. No matter what you planned before the event, it can quickly go right out the window when this factor starts to put pressure on you.

This factor can be extremely powerful when played the right way. The more scarcity you can create, the more valuable it will be in the eyes of others.

**Language**

Your choice of words also has a great deal of influence on other people. Because we are social creatures, at least 60% of our daily lives is spent on oral communication. By choosing words that appeal to the ears of your target, you can capture their attention and bring your story to life. Words can generate a powerful source of energy and convince people to respond to your message. By the same token, the wrong words can crush all of your hard work in mere seconds.

The more adept you are at using the spoken word, the more persuasive you will be. While body language makes up the lion's share of our communication skills, do not underestimate the power of your words. They have a direct impact on the beliefs, attitudes, and perceptions of those around us. Used in the wrong way, you could lose a lot more than you bargained for. Even newscasters are specifically trained to use certain inflections in their voices to project a sense of authority and knowledge.

Elements of voice control also influence people. Consider how you emphasize words, your pitch, pace, fillers, volume, articulation and even where you pause when you speak. Even your lack of words has power. Knowing when to speak and when to let the silence have power says a lot about your own level of confidence.

**Creating Contrast**

Contrast is usually something that is better understood in art, but when applied in persuasion can literally bond someone to you with little effort. When you present someone with two scenarios that seem like they are worlds apart you are creating a contrast. Imagine realizing that you need thousands of dollars to redecorate your home, and then later learning that most of the cost can be eliminated by using a different designer. This is creating contrast. Chances are you will feel indebted to the new designer or contractor that saved you all the money, even if you later learn that none of the other expenses you thought you needed were even necessary.

They key to the success of using contrast is to use the two scenarios close together. If too much time is allowed to pass before the favorable option is presented, contrast loses much of its power. Because people will naturally be drawn to positive news, when they hear negative reports they are usually emotionally thrown. Here, timing is key. If you submit your concept in quick succession with another great idea, your message will have little impact. There is not enough contrast between the two ideas. However, if you submit your idea immediately after someone else presents a bad idea, the power of your message will cut right to the heart of the listeners and you will see an immediate reaction.

**Creating Expectations**

Many people make decisions based on what they know others will expect them to do. We see this often in children. If the parents expect them to behave poorly in a given situation, they will usually oblige them. The same is true of all of us. If your target is aware of your expectations, they will usually act accordingly.

People have all sorts of ways to show what they expect of you. Some will tell you directly what they want and others will use more subtle means. For example, if you are meeting someone for the first time, how you introduce yourself lets them know exactly how you want to be addressed. If you use your title and surname, then they know you want to be addressed that way. However, if you tell them a nickname or just a first name, they are more likely to feel more at ease and comfortable around you. The casualness of your words can put them at ease.

Whenever you communicate with others, you're letting them know what your expectations are.

**Involvement**

You have much more influence over another person when they are involved in what you are doing or saying. Efforts to engage the other person requires you to tap into their sensory perceptions. We all have five senses that is continually feeding the brain. The more of these senses we are able to engage in, the more involved and committed to you the other person will be. By creating a very specific atmosphere you can yield a powerful influence over them.

Just talking to the other person is not sufficient enough to influence people because listening is merely a passive exercise. It doesn't evoke any emotions or connection. However, if the other person is listening, smelling, tasting, and feeling all at the same time, it would be nearly impossible for their mind to drift off and focus on something else.

There are several ways you can create a sense of involvement in the other person. If you're in a discussion with them, make sure the conversation is not one-sided. Ask information questions that will naturally compel them to contribute to the discussion. You can engage their creative mind by telling stories designed to touch them emotionally. By creating an atmosphere of suspense, you can keep them hanging on to your every word until you achieve your set goal. The more involved a person is in your goal the more likely they will do whatever is necessary to give you what you want.

**Build Self-Esteem**

One might think that a person with a weak self-esteem is easy to manipulate but that would not be entirely correct. The general belief is that anyone that is lacking in self-esteem craves acceptance. The reality though is that acceptance, praise, and recognition is a common need shared by all of us. It speaks to the core of what it means to be human.

Watch what happens when you praise anyone, even with the smallest and most insignificant expressions. You can literally see their spirits lift and their mood change. All humans need praise and recognition. In fact, it is the only way a person gets built up psychologically over time. Praise from others satisfies our need to be a part of something bigger than ourselves.

When persuading others, presenting your message in a way that edifies your listeners will take you much farther than you might imagine. The more you build them up, the more they will be inclined to follow you through to your goal. This rule is true for everyone regardless of their level of self-esteem. But the mere fact that self-esteem is key to their connection with you, your goal should be making your listener feel needed and respected.

You will have to walk a fine line here though. There is a big difference in helping to build someone's self-esteem and boosting someone's ego. So, don't go overboard when it comes to this practice. Make sure you understand the difference because this quality could easily backfire on you.

**Association**

As social beings, our brains subconsciously look for connections in everything we do. We do this so quickly we rarely recognize that we have automatically categorized people as soon as we make a connection. These categories instantly put some people closer to us and others far away. We categorize based on a myriad of options. We might decide where they fit in our lives based on the colors they wear, the people they are with, the jobs they have, the music they listen to, or even emotions they express. We use these associations to make judgments about them and how deep our relationship with them will be.

When you are trying to apply your powers of persuasion you utilize this internal and instinctive need to create the type of relationship you need. You can tap into it to bring out certain emotions you need them to employ to bond them to you. Obviously, everyone's idea of association will be different so before you can use the art of association, you need to learn enough about that person to figure out what kind of associations you need.

**Balance**

When you are manipulating your target, your focus needs to be on their emotions but that does not mean that you can neglect their ability to reason on things. There has to be some level of balance in order to get your desired results. You may be able to evoke a powerful emotional response that may last for a while but no one can maintain intense emotions all the time. By the same token, you may be able to use careful reasoning and logic analyzing a certain situation but that will eventually become boring and they may lose interest.

Emotions can stimulate a person to action, generating the necessary energy to move them in the direction you want them to go. Logic works by laying a foundation they can rely on to make their decisions. By creating a careful balance between the two, you can create the perfect environment for evoking the right response.

To become a master manipulator, you will need all of these qualities, but you will use them each to different degrees depending on your target. Everyone needs them in order to tailor their message for the best results.

## 7 Qualities That Signify the Perfect Target

With the above qualities, just about anyone can be manipulated. However, there are some people that will stand out as the perfect target for persuasion. These people will show some express vulnerabilities that will be easy to identify.

*The need to please:* Some people crave attention so much that they will be more than eager to please others. This may stem from a need to be accepted or a low self-esteem, but these people are pretty easy to pick out from a crowd. Push just a few of their buttons and they will usually fall in line pretty quickly.

*Fishers of compliments:* Along with that need to please, many will also be constantly fishing for compliments. In other words, they will constantly be creating scenarios where they will earn praise and approval from those around them.

*Fear of their own negative emotions:* They will fight very hard not to display any sign of negativity in their lives. They may resist the tendency to express disapproval of something they seek, their disappointment, frustration or anger. They will apply avoidance techniques in order to not show that they feel uncomfortable about a given situation. They may work hard to find the right words to say what you want to hear in order to not lose their connection with you.

*Lack of assertiveness:* Assertiveness is one's ability to feel self-assured and confident about themselves and to have the kind of control that keeps them from being aggressive and overpowering others. People who are assertive do not need to demand or force others to do things. They have a quiet and controlled demeanor that naturally draws people on. However, those who lack assertiveness are very unsure of themselves, struggle with saying no to anyone even when they are uncomfortable about the situation making them the ideal target for manipulation.

*No clear personal boundaries:* Those who are willing to compromise on their personal boundaries can make easy targets for manipulation. They lack an established sense of identity and therefore are inclined to bend to the whims of others. When anyone is not clear on who they are or what they should stand for, they tend to stand for everything. They have no firm grounding to base their decisions on and therefore are easily swayed.

*Low self-reliance:* They lack independence and therefore are always in need of help from others. In essence, they are always in need of other people to help them get through even the most basic things in life. They struggle to survive if someone is not there to provide the basic necessities for them.

*Belief in their own self-control:* Sometimes referred to as locus of control, it does not reference one's level of control over certain events but rather to one's belief that they have control. This is a very big difference. When one believes that outside factors have more control over a situation than they do it leaves them open to all sorts of persuasions.

A person that believes he has control will more likely believe that anything he does has in some way been caused by him. When something goes wrong, he'll accept the blame rather than shifting it to someone else. However, if he believes that the fault lies in external factors, he will likely not want to take responsibility even if it is pointed out that he is responsible.

Any one of these qualities will make a person a pretty easy target for manipulation. In most cases, they won't be hard to find, they may even have a form of nervous behavior that will put their low self-esteem on display. An effective manipulator should first take the time to observe potential targets and look for these specific characteristics to identify them.

## The Targets That are Harder to Win Over

No matter how careful you are in choosing your targets, there will inevitably come a time when you're going to find someone who resists your attempts to manipulate them. It's true, everyone will fall for the strategies of manipulation at one time or another, even those who you might feel are relatively wise. However, there are those few that will not succumb to your attempts no matter what you do. Trying to influence these targets can literally leave you with a headache as you struggle to overcome their resistance.

However, there are those who have been "burned" before by past manipulators. So, while you may be able to overcome their objections, their defenses will be up and they will be on guard for any other possible forms of influence.

Think about it. A common manipulation strategy is to promise them relief from whatever stresses or worries they are trying to overcome. However, those who have been burned have a highly suspicious nature and will question everything, even seeing ulterior motives in your efforts. You will have to work pretty hard to overcome those objections.

Their past baggage will cause them to approach every new relationship with an anticipation that something is wrong. It will take a lot of work to get them to believe in any promises you make, no matter how reasonable you sound. They may even insist on solid evidence, physical proof, or even more time for you to show that you are worth the trust you are asking for.

Another person you may have trouble reaching are those who are "loners." It is human nature to find a place within a social network. The common and often unspoken belief that there is safety in numbers is what makes a person an easy target. People who are loners, content with their own company have somehow overcome that need and are less likely to succumb to the same tactics that others may follow.

A person who is not part of a family, team, religion, or tied to any other group does not feel the need or is resistant to inclusion. While this is a natural inclination that we are all born with, they have learned to survive without it. In order to reach those people, you will have to rekindle that need in them in order to get them on your side.

A good manipulator seeks out weaknesses and works at them until they can trigger an emotional reaction. Your main goal is to get them so emotionally involved that they develop a sort of tunnel vision that gets them to push their own logical reasoning ability aside and respond emotionally to your needs. In essence, you are creating a narrow-minded focus in them, so they only see what you want them to see.

Those people who are resistant are strong willed enough to carefully think through every scenario will be your most difficult targets. They may actually be manipulators themselves and will therefore recognize your tactics as soon as you apply them. It doesn't mean that they can't be overcome with these strategies, but you will likely have to work longer and harder to get them to where you want them to be.

It's true, there are some targets that will seem impervious to your efforts, but don't let that discourage you. Where you can't find success with one person there are plenty others that you will be able to influence.

# Chapter Four: Decoding Body Language

Communication is much more than just words. Inside of all of us there is a hidden code that we inherited at birth that allows us to communicate even when words are not available. In fact, this hidden form of language is far more reliable than the words we choose to speak. Through it, we let others know how we are feeling, what we are thinking, and our innermost desires.

Body language is more than just gesturing because its roots are embedded deep in our subconscious. One movement can relay more meaning than a thousand words strung together, no matter how poignant. Still, few of us have learned how to read this language and use it to our advantage. We are often so focused on the verbal message people are delivering that we fail to notice what is right in front of our eyes.

This form of non-verbal communication is done on a subconscious level and the messages others are sending to you can be very valuable to a manipulator. Not only can you read and interpret what others are saying, you can learn from your own actions what kind of messages you are sending out. Either way, understanding the underlying mean of these body signals can give you a wealth of information that will make it easier to create a persuasive strategy you can rely on.

Reading the Body's Subtle Signals

There are two kinds of body language cues you can look for: positive and negative. Positive body cues tell you if the person is feeling confident about what he is saying or comfortable in his surroundings. You will see them in all sorts of settings so whether you're talking one to one or you're in a group, these will easily be observed.

- Standing erect with head high and shoulders back
- Making good eye contact and smiling eyes
- Comfortably gesturing with hands and arms while engaged in conversation
- Speaks clearly with a moderate tone of voice
- Nodding his head to indicate is listening and interested in the conversation

Negative body cues are an indication that there is some level of discomfort either with you or with the setting. Look out for these signs:

- Avoiding eye contact
- Minimal hand or arm gestures. They keep their arms close to the body as if in a defensive mode.
- No nodding or smiling while listening or when speaking
- Arms folded across the body – this tells you they are closed off or are unwilling to accept what is happening.
- Nervous tapping of hands or feet
- Clenched fists
- Speaks quickly or at a high pitch

There are signs that may not relay comfort or confidence, but rather how interested a person may be in your message. Recognizing these can help to determine if you are really reaching a person or if your words are falling on deaf ears.

- If they're head is down and there is no eye contact it usually indicates a lack of interest
- Signs of active listening or concentrating on what is being said involves getting the whole body involved in the conversation. Signs of active listening:
    - Repeating or paraphrasing your words

- Leaning forward or to the side while listening
- Slight tilt of the head or if sitting, resting the head on one hand
- Mirroring your facial expressions
- Steepling the fingers – sign of authority and control

When there is a lack of interest, you will see other signs.

- They may be easily distracted
- Constantly checking the time
- Doodling
- Playing with their hair
- Picking at their fingernails
- Not asking questions
- Staring at something else
- Fiddling with small objects

Before you can become a master manipulator you have to become a master at body language. Skillful use of it can help you to decide on the spot whether you need to change tactics or not. It doesn't matter what your goal may be, knowing the message can tell help you to land that perfect job, negotiate the best price, win an argument, or whether you should proceed with a relationship.

It is important to note here that these are the subtle cues founded in modern western culture. Body language signs are not universal and therefore can vary from one culture to the next. If you are not living in the modern western culture like in America, the UK, or Canada, it would be smart to take the time to learn these cues before you attempt regular communication. One gesture in one area could mean something entirely different where you are.

## The Secret Messages of the Face

Our faces are also very expressive sending out messages that words can never convey clearly. We all know about smiles and their meanings, but did you know that there were different types of smiles, each one with its own unique message? A smile can show you're happy, shy, warm, or fake. There is one smile called the "Duchenne" smile that is considered the most genuine of all. It is the one that the corners of your mouth pull upward while you squeeze your eye muscles making crow's feet in the corners. Fake smiles do not have the crow's feet in the corner of the eyes – when you see that, you know that the person is not sincere in his expressions. Fake smiles tend to show more teeth than genuine smiles.

Frowns on the other hand, show disapproval, unhappiness, or doubt. A person may tell you he's feeling good about something but the look on his face could be sending you an entirely different message. Body language can tell you a lot about what someone is feeling but facial expressions tell you clearly how a person is feeling.

Unlike gestures and movements in body language that do not cross cultural boundaries, facial expressions are universal. No matter what background or history a person has these expressions can clearly be seen in every part of the world. Research has even indicated that most of us, without realizing it, make judgments based almost entirely on a person's facial expressions. We conclude that if someone's face reflects joy and happiness, they are more intelligent than someone who is constantly showing anger. This helps us to understand how valuable it can be to learn and understand true facial expressions. It speaks to the core feelings of your target so that know exactly what you are dealing with.

*Eyes:* There is a reason why people have described the eyes as the window to the soul. There is so much expression in them that sometimes people do not have to say a word but their thoughts and feelings come across very clearly. When you are involved in a conversation take the time to observe their eyes. The way they move will give you a glimpse into what's going on in their brain.

- Gazing: When they are making direct eye contact with you, they are showing interest to what you are saying. However, the length of time they gaze can also reflect meaning. Have you noticed how uncomfortable you become if someone gives you prolonged eye contact? That's because we naturally perceive this type of gazing as a threat, much like a predator would feel uncomfortable if a dog was watching you intently.

    Breaking eye contact also shows you that your listener is bored, distracted, or is trying to hide his true feelings about the discussion.

- Blinking: We all blink frequently throughout our waking hours, but when you notice someone blinking too much or not enough, they are sending you an unconscious message. Too few blinks means that they are deliberately controlling their eye movements. Gamblers often do this to resist the temptation to appear too excited about a potential outcome. If you notice rapid blinking it is usually an indication that they are feeling nervous or uncomfortable.

- Pupil size is an amazing sign that most people have no idea they are using. Pupils react to environmental lighting but beyond that, they also reflect emotions in their small changes in size. If they are highly dilated, it could be a sign that they are keenly interested or aroused.

- If they are moving up and to the right when answering a question, it could mean they are lying. Up and to the left usually means they are being honest with you.

- Disgust can be seen when the eyes narrow. It is a negative response and when it is accompanied by tight lips it can mean anger or hostility. Usually the narrower the eyes become the more intense the negative emotion.

- Eye blocking or the covering his eyes after you've made a request usually indicates that they are uncomfortable with something you've just said or that they disagree with your viewpoint.

- Arched eyebrows often show happiness, especially if it is accompanied by a smile or by the pupils getting larger. You will notice mothers do this often when they see their children.

- Fear is also showed with arched eyebrows but is accompanied with wide open eyes and the absence of a smile. There is also a quick and fleeting look and the pupils will dilate as a result of a quick burst of adrenaline flooding the system.

- Probably the most important thing you want to see in the eyes is their focus. When they are keenly interested in your message, their pupils will start to constrict. The opposite is also true, if they are not interested you can expect to see the pupils dilate.

These non-verbal cues can be awesome tools when it comes to reading people's emotions. The next time you are engaged in conversation, start to take notice of these subtle little glimpses into their soul. You will begin to see a whole new world unfold right before you and what you learn can help you to understand exactly what you need to do in order to achieve your goals.

***The Mouth:*** The mouth also says a lot even when the person is not speaking. Every expression has a meaning and learning how to read them is essential for anyone who is looking to persuade someone.

- Covering the mouth: This is usually an attempt to be polite. People do this when they are coughing or sneezing, but they also do it when they are bored or yawning, which could be a warning sign that you need to change tactics. One thing you want to watch out for is covering the mouth as a sign of disapproval.

- Pursed lips: When they tighten the lips, it is a sign of distrust or disapproval of some kind.

- Biting lips: This is a cue that they are worried or stressed about something.

- Turned up at the corners: Indicates that they are happy or optimistic.

- Turned down at the corners means sadness or disapproval. If the gesture is prominent it could mean extreme distaste.

***Gestures:*** Gestures, like the eyes, are usually some of the most obvious signs that reflect a person's inner feelings. We automatically read gestures without giving them a second thought. No one would question the meaning of a wave or pointing or even counting on the figures. Those are quite easy to understand, but there are also cultural gestures that you might encounter. If you've traveled a lot, you'll notice that a gesture in one country does not always translate to gestures in another country. These are common gestures found in the United States.

- *Clenched fists:* in some instances, it could be a reflection of anger. However, if it is made with the arm upraised it usually means solidarity or unity.
- *Thumbs up:* approval
- *Thumbs down:* disapproval
- *Pinching thumb and forefinger together:* This is a sign of approval or saying everything is okay.
- *The V sign:* This sign, made by holding up the index and middle finger in the shape of a V means victory. It some areas it can also mean peace.

**The Extremities:** Arms and legs are excellent communicators. For example, Crossing your legs and turning them away from the other person lets you know that the other person is taking a defensive position and is wary of you. By paying attention to what the extremities are telling you it will be easy to determine if what they are saying is matching their feelings.

- *Crossing the arms:* the person is feeling defensive or is closed off, not willing to open up to you.
- *Hands on hips:* a sign that they are in control. If the posture looks more defiant it could also be a sign of aggression.
- *Hands clasped behind the back:* this gesture could be a sign that they are bored or anxious. Sometimes could be a sign of anger and frustration.
- *Fidgeting or tapping fingers:* When done rapidly, it is a clear sign that they are impatient or frustrated.
- *Crossing legs:* indication that they are closed off or that they need some separateness or privacy.

***Posture:*** Our posture is another way we unconsciously communicate to others, How we hold our bodies can reflect many things from the state of our health to our sense of confidence. There are two types of posture to watch for.

- *Open:* when the trunk of the body is exposed it tells others that they are open and friendly. An open posture usually means that they are willing and ready to comply.
- *Closed:* When the trunk of the body is closed off by stances like hunching forward or crossing the arms the legs, it can be a show of hostility or anxiety. Usually not a friendly gesture.

***Personal Space:*** In America, people take their personal space very seriously. If you stand too close, they are likely to feel very uncomfortable. It is best to maintain a respectable distance between you and the person you're interacting with. A little too close and they will become defensive and wary, a little too far and they are likely to get the sense that you are being closed off and uninterested.

- *Intimate conversations usually require a distance between 6 to 18 inches.* This distance is acceptable for those in a close relationship and allows for more intimacy and private discussion. The close proximity allows for intimate touching, hugging, and whispering.
- *When it is not an intimate discussion but can still be considered a personal relationship such as with family and friends a distance of 1.5 to 4 feet is considered acceptable.* The amount of distance you maintain between the other person reflects on how close the relationship is. The closer you are the more intimate the bond.
- *In social or group settings, maintaining a physical distance of 4 to 12 feet is acceptable.* This is the acceptable distance for personal acquaintants like co-workers and business

associates. When dealing with people who you are unfamiliar with or those you interact with infrequently, it might be best to stay on the further end of the range.
- *Public distance of up to 15 feet is maintained when you don't need to have direct personal contact. For example, when you are giving a presentation or speaking to an audience you wouldn't want to be too close to your listeners. The distance allows you to make brief eye contact with different people in the audience without making them feel like they have been singled out.*

While you won't need to go out with a measuring tape to determine the proper distance to allow for personal space, you can take your cues from those around you. This is especially important when you are dealing with cultures from other countries. For example, personal space in most Asian cultures is not as important as it is in North America. The same is true with those from Latin America. The more you observe this distance the more effective you will be at reaching your target audience.

Understanding body language will naturally make you a better communicator but it will also help you to understand the signals you're sending out into the universe. This is by no means a full selection of possible gestures so it would be a good idea to do additional research on the topic. That said, just by applying these listed here you will be well on your way to understanding what needs to be done to persuade others.

## Understanding Microexpressions

Before, we discussed the importance of facial gestures in understanding communication. However, one area of facial expressions that we are now beginning to get a better grasp on is that of microexpressions. These are involuntary gestures that happen very quickly when a feeling or emotion is first felt. These generally are more reliable than any other facial gesture as they are impulse reactions that the person has no time to think about. They happen quickly and usually occur within the first fractions of a second after the emotion arises generally starting at ½ of a the first second and lasting $1/15^{th}$ and $1/25^{th}$ of a second before fading. Because they appear and disappear so quickly, they are good indicators of any emotion that a person is trying to hide or suppress.

Learning how to detect these microexpressions is key to becoming persuasive but before you can master this skill, you have to understand the dynamics of the human face and what you should be looking for. According to Dr. Paul Ekman, these expressions are pretty universal. Everyone, no matter where they are from, shares at least seven common expressions that have exactly the same meaning. While there are plenty more microexpressions to learn, knowing at least these seven will give you a pretty good picture of the person you are dealing with and what to expect.

**Surprise:** This common expression is seen by the raising of the upper eyelids, the eyebrows raised and curved. You should also see the mouth partially open when the jaw drops but the lips and mouth muscles will remain relaxed. The length of this expression tells you if the person is surprised or fearful. If it lasts longer than a second it is more likely a sign of fear.

**Fear:** Similar to surprise, fear can be seen when the upper eyelids are raised up. The eyebrows are lifted and pulled together making a flat line. The mouth opens slightly and the lip muscles are tensed and pulled back tightly.

**Disgust:** This classic look is easy to recognize by the wrinkles that form around the nose. The eyebrows are drawn down and the eyes narrow. The upper lid, cheek muscles, and the lower lip are tensed into a sneer making the teeth visible.

**Anger:** When a person is angry both the upper and lower eyelids are drawn tightly together. The eyebrows are pulled down in the center and drawn together tightly. You'll see vertical lines appear between the eyebrows and the eyes themselves take on a strong stare or start to bulge out. Some people have a habit of thrusting the jaw forward when they are extremely angry.

**Happiness:** This emotion is seen when both sides of the mouth pull up in the corners making a symmetrical smile. Many people try to pretend to be happy by forcing a smile but you should be able to tell the difference by looking at the corners of the eye. Genuine happiness also shows in the eyes as well as the mouth. Look for the corner eye muscles to engage showing the tell-tale signs of crow's feet. Expect to see more engagement of the face muscles when happiness is genuine than you will with a forced display of emotion.

**Sadness:** This feeling can be seen when the corner muscles of the lips pull down at the sides and the lower lip juts out in a pout. You may also see the inside corner of the eyebrows lift slightly.

**Contempt:** This emotion can be clearly identified by the classic raising of one side of the mouth making a sneer or a smirk.

Microexpressions are universal and common. They differ from regular expressions in that they are very difficult to intentionally create. People can readily hide their innermost feelings with regular facial gestures but microexpressions are formed in a different part of the brain and are impulse reactions. They are fleeting at best and disappear as quickly as they come so to notice them and identify them will require you to pay very close attention to your target so you can catch that one instant that will reveal everything you need to know.

What Walking Styles Say About Someone

Most of us do not spend a lot of time worrying about how a person walks but a recent study published in *Social Psychological and Personality Science,* gives us good reason to consider it. The study conducted in 2017 by a health and wellness expert at Maple Holistics reveal that one's walking speed could tell us at least five different personality traits. These traits: agreeableness, openness, extraversion, conscientiousness, and neuroticism can tell us a lot about the kind of people we are dealing with.

There is a great deal to be learned when you analyze their speed, stride, and how they hold their arms when they are walking. By analyzing these characteristics, you can reveal something about them that you may not otherwise be able to pick up.

**Fast Walkers:** People who walk fast tend to be more outgoing and maybe even more conscientious. In fact, the faster they walk the more outgoing they tend to be.

**Slow Walkers:** Those who move at a slower pace reflect a more cautious personality. When they take shorter strides at a more leisurely pace it could reflect a little bit of me-ism as they are classic signs of a self-centered personality. However, this does not necessarily mean that it is a bad thing. It simply reflects a person who is looking out for his own best interests. Those who are more introverted may also walk slow but their body language reveals a lack of confidence. They keep their head down and pull into themselves. A cautious person is not an introvert but rather more careful about his decisions. He walks with his head held high so he can see and analyze everything in his environment.

**Veering to the Left:** People who gradually veer to the left as they walk tend to be showing signs of anxiety and stress. The further they veer off the straight path the more anxiety they are feeling. No one fully understands this phenomenon but it is believed that the right side of the brain is more fully engaged in solving problems or dealing with their worries or fears than the left side.

**The Saunter:** When someone takes a more leisurely stroll, literally sauntering down their path with their head held high but no clear destination in sight it is a powerful sign of confidence. These people fall into a slow and easy stride reflecting the calm state of mind.

**Energetic Walker:** Those who move with a high energy in their step are super conscientious and are more detail oriented. They walk quickly even when covering short distances. For instance, they may move just a few steps to a chair or across the room. Their gait is quick but it is not smooth. Their movements will be jerking as they switch their attention from one thought to the next.

**Graceful Walkers:** Graceful walkers reflect a quiet and inner sense of confidence, but how you read them will depend on the direction their feet are pointed. When their feet are pointing outwards as they walk it is a sign of high self-esteem. This position is not a natural gait but is one that is taught. Toes pointing inward is a sign of insecurity.

**Slumped Shoulders:** If their posture has them in a slightly bent forward position with their shoulders hunched over it is a classic sign of discomfort. It is a position that is designed to protect the vital organs of the body. They may have suffered some sort of trauma in their past either physically or psychologically but have not yet recovered.

When it comes to body language, the more you learn the more you realize that every movement, every nuance, and every slight little twitch or gesture is working like a mirror to the reflecting what is going on in the mind and the hearts of the people you are interacting with. While learning these things won't make you a mind reader, you can get pretty close to it when you apply them to your art of persuasion.

# Chapter Five: Essential Manipulation Tools

The art of manipulation has a very specific goal. You want to change the mind of your target so that you can affect the kind of behavior you want to see. Learning how to read other people and detect their emotional state of mind is only half the battle. Once you understand your target it's time to select the proper manipulation tools to use to your advantage.

There are several different approaches that are very effective in persuading people. The ones included in this chapter work subtly on the subconscious mind so the target never fully realizes what's happening, but they yield the best results.

Everyday Manipulation Tricks

**Foot in the Door:** The main principle behind this concept is to get someone to do what you want them to do. In essence you are laying the groundwork to ask for a favor. It starts small by asking for a smaller and less important favor first. By doing this, you're building a small but simple connection between the two of you based on an unwritten rule of commitment that you can fall back on later.

The Chinese have been practicing this strategy for centuries. It follows that by doing small but insignificant favors for someone over time causes them to be indebted to you. It's like putting money in the bank so you can make a bigger request later on. While in China, this tool runs much deeper than in western society, it is a powerful weapon in indebting someone to you.

A good example of how this can be used can be seen can be seen in all walks of life. For example, you might find yourself in unfamiliar territory and ask someone for directions. This simple request creates a connection with you. After a simple and brief conversation, you might make your second request by explaining that you're not very good with directions so would rather they showed you instead of telling you. The person may decide to draw you a map or even personally walk you to your destination. There is a good chance of this working if you asked for the smaller favor first. However, if you had just approached a stranger and asked them to walk you to your destination, you almost certainly would have been unsuccessful.

This theory was tested by researchers back in 1966. A group of 156 women were divided into four groups. They started by asking the first three groups to answer a few basic questions about the kitchen products they used. After several days, they asked permission to go through their kitchen so they could catalogue the products they used. The fourth group was only asked the second question. The results showed the effectiveness of this approach with a 52.8% success rate for the first three groups and only a 22.2% success rate for the fourth one.

You can see this applied everywhere you look in marketing. Most online websites start by asking something that doesn't seem to cost you anything. They may ask you for your email address and then later ask for something bigger. Someone may ask you to "like" a page and then later ask you for a comment, which could later lead to a sale.

***Door in the Face***: The main principle behind this technique is to ask for something extremely big and unreasonable and then when declined, ask for something smaller. It works on the opposite scale of the Foot in the Door technique. In this case, you are requesting something so large that you know you're going to be refused and then you make a request for something that is much easier for them to comply with.

A case in point would be if you asked a friend for a large loan and then when refused, ask for a significantly smaller one. This works primarily because just by making the initial request, you have moved your relationship up to another level causing them to feel some sort of obligation to you. Then it becomes much easier for them to comply with your second request without hesitation.

This fact was verified in a case study performed in the retail market. Researchers used one saleswoman who was selling cheese to people in the Austrian Alps. She first offered hikers passing by two pounds of cheese for eight euros, and when they rejected the sale, she then downgraded her request by offering one pound for four euros. The results were impressive with only a 9% success rate with the first request and a 24% success rate after the second.

*Anchoring:* The main thought behind anchoring is to create a cognitive bias by creating familiarity with the same or a similar product so your target can make a decision based on this knowledge. There are several ways you can apply this technique from marketing to landing that dream job you want.

It works similar to the Foot in the Door technique. Stores often raise the price of certain products by 15% prior to a 10% sale. People see the price at a discount from the actual posted price not realizing that they are paying even more for the product than they would have before the sale.

Evidence that this works was seen in a study where 100 subjects were given three different options for subscriptions. The first option was an online cost of $59, the second option was for a printed subscription for $125, and a third option was for print and web combination for $125. The results showed that out of the 100 subjects only 16 chose the first option and 84 chose the third option. Then the second option was removed and the same exercise was given to another 100 subjects where only 32 chose the third option with the remaining 68 choosing the first.

The results showed that when option B was a factor it was merely used as an anchor. No one would seriously consider it, but it clearly showed the value of the other two options. This process is an effective means of transferring learning experiences. It its core, it gives people a stimulus or a personal experience from which to base their decisions on.

***Commitment & Consistency:*** The basic principle here is to tap into your target's internal sense of consistency. As creatures of habit, if you are able to get them to commit to something small and insignificant, then you can use that to motivate them to do something more in the future.

All of us do this to some degree in real life. When we go shopping, we buy the same products we are familiar with, we take the same route to work every day, and we usually eat the same things with few variations in every meal. Because of this internal need for consistency, we rarely try things new. By getting someone to do something for you once you start a precedent that they will follow to maintain consistency.

Many online websites use this principle in their marketing efforts. They start by asking potential customers to sign up for regular emails from their company. You've seen them on the screen when you visit their sites with words like "Yes, I like free money," or "Yes, I want to know more." Sometimes they will even give you options that make you feel like you have to choose one over the other. For example, you may be given two options, "Yes, I want to know more about how to make option," and "No, I don't want to be successful." The second option is so far from the truth that you feel compelled to choose the first one. But once you've made the decision, no matter how insignificant, you will feel obligated to stick to it.

To get the best results, the first commitment should be easy to make. It won't cost them much or anything at all. A charity may send out a petition to get people to increase their commitment to their efforts. The initial cost is minimal at best. Later, they can ask for larger donations and most will comply just to keep their level of commitment involved.

**Social Proof:** We've all heard of peer pressure, right? Social proof is a perfect example of peer pressure at work. The prevailing principle here is that you don't want to be the odd man out. This concept is based on the thought that before anyone makes a decision, they will stop and think about what decision their peers will make and will usually act accordingly.

If you are working in a restaurant and there is an empty tip jar present, you could start the tips coming in by adding the first coins of your own. Customers are much more likely to add to a jar that already has money in it than to be the first to get the ball rolling. You are more likely to leave a comment on an article or video if you see others are doing it as well.

A 1935 case study bears this out. Researchers took several subjects and placed them in a dark room with the only source of light a pinpoint 15 feet away. They were asked to watch the light and give an estimate to how much that light moved. Each participant gave different answers about the movement.

The second day of the study, they were put into groups and asked the same question. This time they all came to a singular agreement that was far removed from the estimates they gave just the day before.

***Authority:*** We learn from an early age to listen to those who have authority. Regardless of the area of expertise, establishing yourself as an authority on a subject will have a powerful influence on others.

Marketing experts use this very effectively with phrases like "9 out of 10" doctors approve this medication. Or they may say something like "our product won 8 out of 10 awards for being the best." Websites and blogs often enlist the endorsement of recognized authorities in their area of expertise, or they post testimonials from past customers to give evidence that they are the professionals they claim to be.

One Yale University psychologist proved this very effectively in a series of studies called the Milgram Experiment. The studies consisted of three different people, the experimenter, the teacher, and the learner.

The teacher's role was to ask the learner questions. If the learner gave a wrong answer, the teacher would give them an electric shock. The experimenter then would press the teacher to continue to use the electric shock even if there was evidence that the learner was in pain.

In the majority of the cases, the teacher would continue to administer pain even they it went against their conscience. In fact, 8 out of 10 teachers would continue to give the electric shocks regardless of the circumstances. This gives evidence that most people are willing to cross even a moral boundary if their instructions are given by someone in authority.

***Scarcity:*** The fear of missing out is a powerful one and it is the principle that scarcity is built on. People use it to create a sense of urgency and compel their targets to make a decision sooner rather than later. In reality, the tendency to want something when it is in short supply is very strong so by convincing someone that soon something is going to run out within a certain amount of time is more likely to drive them to buy it.

Scarcity is probably one of the most often used persuasion techniques in the world today. We see it used in marketing, in relationships, and in the social world. If you've ever tried to book a vacation online, you'll probably be greeted with there are only a few seats left on this flight, or this offer expires at midnight, or you can only buy these at this time a year. The whole premise is what America's Black Friday is based on.

In one study, 180 student subjects were separated into two groups. The first group was given a product and told of its scarcity while the second group was told that there was an abundant supply. The result showed that most subjects were eager to buy simply because they were afraid that it would no longer be available.

A classic example of this is a case discussed by psychiatrist of a car salesman who made it a point to have several people show up for a car at the same time. This created an aire of competition and anxiety between them making the actual car seem more valuable than it really was.

When used successfully, there is unique sense of power for the victor. The theory is that this principle protects one sense of freedom to choose. Whenever freedom of choice is limited, we have an inborn desire to protect it. By increasing scarcity, we instinctively recognize that our access to that item is restricted unless we do something quickly.

***Reciprocation:*** Reciprocation is the act of obligating one to you because of something you've done for them. Regardless of what the gift is, just the act of giving it generates a powerful need to return the favor. We automatically feel indebted to the giver and the manipulator can definitely use it to their advantage.

This can be used in a wide variety of ways. For example, you might offer a free gift for the first contributors to your cause or you could be given a free download of a book before being asked to make a larger purchase.

Evidence bears this out in a study conducted at a New York city restaurant where the waiter would give a small gift before providing the bill. In most cases, this saw an 18% increase in tips. In a similar setting, when the waiter would leave a mint and then walk away, turn around, and give them an additional piece the increase in tips went up to 21%.

These are not the only persuasion techniques there are but they are the most commonly used. Use these to lay the groundwork for your next persuasion strategy and see how much your power of influence will increase.

## 11 Persuasion Tricks to Start Getting What You Want in Everyday Life

We live in a dog eat dog world. It doesn't matter who or where you are, you will fall into one of two classes: the manipulator or the one being manipulated. We call them mind games and they are being played out all around us. You need to know them just to make sure that you're not caught in the latter group. Not that being manipulated is always a bad thing, but at least if you are being manipulated you know and recognize the signs and you can then use them to your advantage.

Once you learn these persuasion tricks, you'll be able to use them to get everything you want out of life.

1. **Hardly Evil:** By helping someone else to achieve their own goals you make them indebted to you. The general concept that we all believe in is that you can get what you want from life as long as you help other to achieve their own goals.
2. **A Little Manipulative:** Asking for favors in a more public setting can make people feel more inclined to do things for you. Rather than asking in a more private setting, making a public request is less likely to be turned down.
3. **Bait and Switch:** Using a decoy offer to hook people then offering them something of higher value, and then making a final offer that seems to be of the same value but less effective in order to get them to purchase what you want.
4. **Focus on the Win:** Get your target to realize what he is gaining in the deal rather than what he is losing.
5. **Mirroring:** Mirror the other person's body language to get them to be comfortable with you. They are more likely to connect with you and do what you want.
6. **Watching:** Make them feel as if they are watched. This can be done by showing them an image of eyes. Subconsciously, when we see eyes as in an image or in a video, they will feel as if they are being judged, which will make them alter their behavior to something they feel will be more accepted.
7. **Tap Into Insecurities:** Your choice of words can tap into how they feel about themselves. People tend to think more of their personal identifies when they hear nouns but they think more of their behavior when they hear verbs. If you want to tap into their insecurities, choose more nouns in your conversations than verbs and you'll weaken their defenses.
8. **Deception:** Speak rapidly if you want them to agree with you. Use lots of words to overwhelm them so they will lower their

guard. Many times, they will agree with you because they just can't keep up.
9. **Scheming:** Approach them at the end of the day when they are tired and ready to quit. When people are exhausted, they're more likely to comply with your request because their energy to resist is pretty much spent.
10. **Fear:** Tapping into their fears is an effective way to get people to comply with your request. Expose their fears and then immediately offer a solution.
11. **Confusion:** Deliberately confuse them. Most people's pride won't allow them to admit that they don't fully understand. The easiest response for them is to agree. Offering prices in unfamiliar terms will make them give up because they struggle to mentally process it.

## How to Use the Six Laws of Persuasion

The laws of persuasion are constantly in use all around us. It is at the core of every business negotiation, every relationship discussion, every parent-teacher or parent-child debate, and the center of every social media interaction. It is a fact of life that is essential for every one of us whether we're in business or not. Every one of these aspects employs skill negotiations on some level.

To be successful at using these laws, you need to first understand yourself (your EQ) and the goals you want to achieve, but you also need to understand what's in the heart of your target. This will create a platform from which you can launch your influence over others and affect the kind of change you want to see in your world.

But successful manipulation should not be just about what you want. While you will be able to gain a modicum of success thinking only of yourself, your best results will come when you create a situation that will be mutually beneficial for both you and your target. How well you do this will determine the extent of your success and how efficiently you can ensure that all parties are winners in your negotiations. To do this, you need to develop your expertise in employing the six main laws of persuasion.

We don't realize it, but the average person makes around 35,000 decisions every day. Of course, the majority of these choices are made on the subconscious level and therefore do not require any conscious thought. They provide us with ways to simplify our lives, gives us shortcuts, and are designed to save us either time and/or money. However, it is those conscious decisions we all must make that will allow us to have influence over others and give us what we want. Here is where the six laws of persuasion can hold sway. We talked briefly about them in the last section, but we're going to examine them a little more closely here.

***Law of Reciprocity:*** The law of reciprocity compels others to return favor for favor. By giving someone something they will feel obligated to repay you. To increase this sense of gratification, if you make sure you give them something, they want their connection to you will be even stronger.

Applying this in your life could be pretty simple. Keep in mind though that getting someone to agree to something without asking for something in return sets a pretty bad precedent that will cause the other person feel entitled and you feeling at a loss. By giving them something it gives them a sense of having some bargaining power. So, using a quid-pro-quo works best and can help to establish a longer standing relationship. The sooner you create this understanding, the easier it will be to persuade that person again and again. It is an extremely effective way of bringing your target into your fold and closing the deal whatever it is.

***Law of Commitment and Consistency:*** Using consistency as a means of easing your targets discomfort is important. Once you've established a relationship with that person, it's important that you stick to it and not deviate. Showing the other person that you are committed to a decision (no matter how significant) gives them the assurance that you are not going to abandon them at the first sign of change. Salespeople are very good at this. By getting their customers to agree on several smaller things one right after another they set a precedent of commitment. So, when they do ask for the big sale, it is almost impossible for them to say no.

***Law of Liking:*** Whether you want to attract another person and kindle a new relationship or you're looking to land that dream job of yours, you will probably use the Law of Liking. This basic law of human nature dictates that we are drawn to those people who are more like ourselves. The more similarities you find with someone else the deeper your desire to want to please them. When applying the Law of Liking work to establish a good rapport and make it clear that you are like two peas in a pod. The more similarities you can show them the deeper the bond will be. This works well with home-based sales parties, religious groups, and social groups. Remember the old saying, 'birds of a feather flock together.' Once you've made this type of connection with them, the less likely they will want to disappoint you by saying no.

***Law of Scarcity:*** You don't necessarily have to have a limited supply of something to make the fundamental law of scarcity work for you. You can apply the same pressure without it. You could let the other party know that you will be available to answer questions for a limited time only. This works well for seasonal offerings or things only available during a certain time of the year. You just have to create the idea that something is scarce to get the result so they believe that if they hesitate, they may miss out on the privilege entirely.

***Law of Authority:*** When applying this law, it is important that the other person knows that you are the "expert" in this field or you are acknowledged and recommended by recognized experts. This can be done in several different ways. Marketers often use the "testimonials" of past customers, bloggers use the credibility of other more well-known bloggers, and there is certainly nothing wrong with advertising or posting your own credential that establish you as a knowledgeable person in your area of interest.

***Law of Social Proof:*** The dynamics is any social group is quite powerful. It can be quite unnerving to go against the crowd so people are more inclined to conform when necessary. Once people understand what is the accepted behavior in any social group, they are rarely inclined to go against it. Think about how you feel when you are in an unfamiliar social setting. Your first instinct is to look around you to see what other people are doing and then you copy them. Establishing a set of guidelines for your social group will almost always end in conformity that will be difficult for anyone to break.

## All You Need to Know About Reverse Psychology

You've probably heard about using reverse psychology to get people to do things. The principle is very simple. You tell them something opposite of what you want and if they are resistant to your efforts, they will usually do what you desire. The tactic can be quite successful in many different forms of persuasion. However, while simple, it can backfire on you in a pretty big way.

Part of the reason for this is its simplicity. In fact, it is so simple that many will begin to rely on this strategy far too much. Once people begin to understand what you're doing, it can leave a pretty sad taste in their mouth. As a result, you may find that rather than connecting more people to you, it could end up pushing them away leaving a string of broken relationships in its wake. If you do decide to use reverse psychology, make sure that you use it only on rare occasions and not as a regular habit and even then, only in the most serious of situations.

That said, here are some simple ways to use this strategy to get what you want.

***To Change Someone's Mind:*** To do this you have to think beyond the idea of changing the person's mind. Before you can begin, you have to implant your ideas into their head. Even if it is something you know they are resistant to they need to at least recognize the idea as an option.

- **The set-up:** start by presenting the two options they must choose from. For example, we have two options for dinner on Saturday night. If you know that your target has an affinity for Japanese food but you're more interested in Italian you already know what their preference will be.

    Casually present your idea in a matter-of-fact sort of way. You might say something like, "Did you know that there is a new Italian restaurant opening up on Fifth Street this week?"

    When you present your option downplay it to create a negative effect. "I've heard it's pretty good but it'll probably be packed by the time we get there. We might have to wait an hour or more to get a table."

- **Subtle Enticement:** Find subtle ways to build a desire in them. You could happen to have a menu from the new restaurant to look over. Point out some pictures and dishes that you would like to try. You could even start with an Italian night to see if you can imitate true Italian food. This will help them to see just how flavorful Italian food could actually be.

You could also make everything else sound more appealing. Talk about past experiences in Italian restaurants, pleasant memories about the Italian culture, and how "real" Italian food should taste.

- **Add Non-Verbal Cues:** A few days before, start by adding in a few visual images about Italian culture. You could drive by the restaurant on the way home to plant the idea of going there. "It doesn't look as crowded as I thought it would be." Take them for a walk in the area where they can get a whiff of the aromas as they are wafting through the air.

- **Take the Opposing Viewpoint for the Choice You Want:** Once you realize that you have caught their interest, don't give up too quickly but be slightly argumentative. This will compel them to push harder for what they want. This works much better than immediate capitulation. When a person has the natural tendency to resist it gives them a sense of fighting for the choices, they make creating a win for them.

When the event arrives, chances are they will already have made their decision. Introduce the subject again by saying something like "What do you want to do? We can go to the Italian restaurant or we can go to the Japanese." If they are still resistant to Italian you can add something like, "We get to eat Japanese all the time so it won't be anything different, but how often do we really eat Italian?"

Finish with "what do you think?" "I can't decide so it's up to you."

- **Closing:** Finally, you want to resist long enough that the other person is forced to decide. While your goal is to get what you want, the other person must think that it's their decision. After you ask your last questions, wait for them to answer. It may create a bit of discomfort but resist the urge to fill in the silence. Your target is also feeling the pressure too so wait it out until they make the choice. If they are a naturally difficult person then in most cases, they will make the decision you want to do.

**When to Use Reverse Psychology:** Reverse psychology doesn't work on everyone. Some people are more likely to respond to a direct request while others will be more contrary. This is why it is so important that you understand the personality of the people you are targeting. They behavior will dictate which persuasive strategy you should use. This strategy works best with people who have a naturally obstinate and stubborn nature. Here are some questions you might want to ask before you decide.

- Do they usually go with the flow?
- Are they independent thinkers?

If they are naturally fluid and agreeable, using reverse psychology will likely backfire on you. But if they are more independent thinkers and are not usually comfortable with the status quo, they are more likely to be the best subjects for reverse psychology.

**Make it Light:** This works well when you're using reverse psychology on children. Keep the topic lighthearted and fun so that they will believe that they're actually smarter than you. Children love that.

For example, you're trying to get your child to clean his room without having to ask him to do it. Start by setting some rules. "Don't start cleaning your room until I've finished cleaning mine." This sentence might start off sounding like that's all he needs for an excuse to "not" clean his room. He'll be happy. But then you will add something like, "I know you're too young to do it right so I'll come in and help you."

Then leave the room and go about your business. In about an hour, you can return to the room "to help" him and you'll most likely find that he has already finished or is well on his way to proving that he's not too young and he can do it on his own.

Using this same tactic with an adult can be similar. Your goal is to allow them to feel as though they are asserting their own independence in the situation. You might be trying to choose between two different TV shows; one may be serious dramatic film and the other could be a light comedy. Your preference is for the drama so you could say something like "I'm not sure I have the emotional stamina for a really serious drama tonight. If your partner is a naturally resistant person, he may want to convince you that you do have the emotional fortitude for it. He may even go as far as he could to prove it. By allowing him to apply a little resistance for a while then you'll most like end up getting exactly what you want.

**Think About What the Other Person Needs:** Whenever you choose to use reverse psychology, you need to consider what the other person needs or wants in the situation. In some cases, you may have to do a little bobbing and weaving before you get him to give up on his goals. Your strategy is not just to apply the opposing viewpoint but to assess of your desire for what you want is strong enough to overpower their need to resist. If you haven't thought this process through your efforts could easily backfire on you.

Your friend may be interested in visiting or driving through a rather seedy part of town that you know is dangerous. If his desire is extremely strong your efforts at reverse psychology may not work.

However, by analyzing the situation first, you could probably find other ways around the challenge.

As you consider the possibilities start by thinking about all the possible arguments you might come up against in the situation. Then think about the end result you want to achieve. Your goal is to help him to see the risks involved in his decision, not necessarily to prove that you are right or smarter. Sometimes reverse psychology will work and sometimes it won't. Possible things you could say.

"I can't tell you what to do and I can't make you do anything that you don't want to do. I pretty sure that the area is dangerous but only you can decide how much risk you're willing to take to get to where you want to go."

Your goal is achieved. Leave the decision in their hands. If you've applied the right amount of pressure, then there is a good chance that he will decide not to go.

Keep in mind that you won't win every argument this way. Reverse psychology works well only on those personalities that are naturally resistant to going with the flow. Strategies do not always turn out the way you expect them too. Occasionally the situation may escalate into an argument and in the heat of the moment you could lose sight of your goals. Try to avoid this and keep reminding yourself of what you're trying to accomplish and you'll find yourself having more successes in this strategy than not.

Remember, this strategy only works in certain situations and should be used subtly and rarely. It is easy, after achieving a few successes, to want to use it as a fall back but that could get you into trouble and could start to create negative inroads in your relationships. Once others realize this is your fallback position it could cause resentment. You have to learn to let the other person have their way sometimes or they may tire of you always having the power of them.

Try to use this type of tactic in situations where there is not much to lose. Don't use it on something that will dampen your relationship over time. For example, use it when deciding on what to eat or what to do for an afternoon at home. Don't use it when deciding on what car or house to buy.

**Never Lose Your Temper:** It is important to stay calm when using reverse psychology. It could easily escalate into arguments where you can become frustrated or feelings can get hurt. This is especially true when dealing with young people. Be patient, it may take a while before they come start to see things from your point of view.

Emotional outbursts are natural so make sure you can handle them yourself before you begin. If the other person loses it, you need to remain calm. All them to finish their outburst before you continue your discussion.

Most important of all, make sure this is not done in extremely serious situations. It could not only backfire but could cause irreparable damage as a result. A good example of this is someone with a serious medical condition who is resistant to going to the doctor. Your partner's resistance could be stronger than his desire to get help and you might find yourself supporting his fears rather than getting him to do what he seriously needs to do.

# Chapter Six: A Master in Every Arena

Manipulation can be a pretty touchy subject these days. Never before in history have, we seen so many people trying to manipulate others to their advantage. People are constantly on guard against salespeople, bloggers, social media gurus, marketing experts and others. Everywhere you look there just seems to be someone who is trying to hold sway against others for their own advantage.

However, to become a master manipulator, you need to cut through all of that chaff and still find ways to get people on your side. It can be quite unsettling when you end up as a victim of some type of dirty negotiation tactics, especially when it's going to cause you to lose months or even years of your hard earned time and money.

Rest assured, if you're not manipulating there's a good chance that you are being manipulated. It's at the heart of every negotiation whether it is getting your two-year old to use the potty or getting your boss to give you a raise. In this chapter, we're going to teach you how to use manipulation strategies in any type of negotiation situation. That way, you can recognize manipulators when they're trying to sway you and you can hone your skills in a way that will turn the table to your advantage.

## How to Secretly Manipulate Your Boss

If you're dealing with a rather difficult boss it can cause a great deal of stress. Difficult bosses are notorious for being die-hard narcissists, playing favorites, and at times even throwing a temper-tantrum or two. These kinds of people leave you feeling insecure and anxious and you end up spending much of your valuable time complaining rather than working towards achieving your own goals.

It's time to change all that. First, you must accept the obvious. Your boss is not going to change no matter how much you yell back or how hard you work to please him. It's because he doesn't want to change. His child-like antics have worked for him so far, so rather than wasting your energy working to get him into a new frame of mind, you need to change your own tactics.

No matter who you want to manipulate, it is important that you understand where they are coming from. You need to find out what is fueling his difficult and challenging behavior. What is he afraid of and what does he want? This goes back to building up your own EQ. You might have to spend some time observing him in his natural habitat in order to fully understand what he secretly wants.

***What are his secret fears and/or desires:*** In nearly every case where a boss is a tyrant, those negative emotions spring from an underlying fear. In fact, desires and fears are the two strongest emotions to deal with. When you look very closely, everyone is either running or hiding from some secret fear that is buried deep in his psyche or they are running to something they secretly want. This is what drives our behavior. Once you understand what these two elements are in your bosses life you place yourself in a position of power. You need what he wants to avoid and you know what he wants to achieve. You can now predict his reaction to any number of situations so you can develop a strategy that will turn the tables in your favor.

Let's take a brief look at some different types of bosses to see how this works:

- The Finger-Pointer: This boss spends his time blaming those who work under him because he is afraid, he doesn't have enough of his own skills to be a success.
- The Egomaniac: usually believes he is perfect in every way. However, a closer look at his work will usually reveal someone who leaves behind a lot of projects that were started but never finished. This person has a strong desire to be loved and admired but secretly feels he is not deserving of any of it. He feels if he loses his control everything will fall apart. He

believes he is just merely an average person trying to pass himself off as being special.

**Become his ally:** Once you know your boss' fears and desires you need to use it to become his ally. You can do this by feeding his desire or shielding him from his fears. By becoming an ally, you are actually taking back the power he is trying to steal from you. It will give you leverage and put you in a position to demand more and likely get what you want and need.

For the boss that spends his time blaming his underlings, you need to learn to control your own emotions and not fight back when his ire is up. People who blame and shout are trying to instill fear in others, when you don't react in fear, he begins to realize that he cannot overpower you in that way. He will calm down.

Once he is calm you can present yourself as his personal problem-solver. Take the initiative and offer to "fix" the problem. When the problem is solved, he will feel like a success and you will gain his trust in the process. After several of these attempts, you will have become one of his most important assets and a tool he will need to achieve his own level of success.

For the egomaniac you will need a lot more strength and intestinal fortitude to withstand the pressure. Try going with the flow so you can fuel his need for employees that are loyal to him. This type of boss needs to feel like he is in control 100% of the time, by following his cues you can smoothly turn a world of chaos into peace and order. If you are good enough at it, you can position yourself as the trusted wingman that he won't want to do without. In time, when he moves up there's a good chance that you will move up at the same time.

Keep in mind that your goal is not to destroy your boss and let him know that he's not manipulating you. That would be counterproductive to your goals. You're trying to use his fears and desires in a way that will support your goals. As a result, you create a win-win situation that you both can gain from. It will relieve much of the stress from work and give you a higher level of job satisfaction.

**The Meeting Hack:** Sometimes your boss is intent on causing you embarrassment in a meeting or he is just set on refusing to hear your viewpoint. In that case, you'll have to prepare a strategy before the next meeting so you can get your point across.

Start by making sure that you have a consensus group before the meeting begins. In other words, find your friends and allies among those who will be attending. If you don't feel you have enough of those on your side, convince your boss to widen the scope and invite more people, make sure your supporters are on that list.

Prep your people and encourage them to support your ideas. When the meeting begins volunteer to be the one to take minutes. That way, you can frame the follow-up to support your ideas. After the meeting, send an email detailing the events of the meeting and make sure it is written to show that a consensus was reached in your favor.

It doesn't really matter what actually happened in the meeting. Based on the principle that most people will follow the flow; people will usually reframe their memory to match what is written in your minutes. However, it is important to make sure that when you submit your minutes, you have at least given some recognition to the points of view of the others in the meeting.

Be prepared if someone does accuse you of changing the flow of the meeting. In your minutes, cover you bases by using phrases like "the general sense of the meeting was...." Or "several alternative suggestions were put forth including...", "there was a difference of opinion on..." "However, there were no major objections to the concept that...." This will show that other ideas and suggestions were considered.

If you think this is an unscrupulous strategy then think again. Go back through your mind to consider how many meetings have already been planned to discuss one issue and in the end, the main topic of discussion was one thing but, in the end, the majority of people ended up discussing something entirely different. It is a common practice in business meetings and you probably thought it was just an accident that it happened. The only difference is now, you know that it was a planned strategy.

**Bury Information:** Another classic strategy for manipulation is to find ways to hide crucial information in order to create a basis for "plausible deniability." Information that may appear detrimental to you or to a case you're working on is, in most cases, essential that you inform your boss. However, there are ways you can do it without getting your or your boss into trouble.

If your boss is like most people, he is constantly on the run. If you give him a stack of papers, he will not likely have the time or the desire to read through them all before giving his signature. By adding the information you are required to report hidden a few pages before the end of the document you're pretty safe that he won't see it. In addition, if you add the document to another report as an attachment.

If your boss does take the time to read it, he's likely just going to give it a cursory glance and then move on to something else. Once he's made his decision, based on the information you made obvious for him to see or he learns of the negative information later, you can honestly inform him that you provided the data in said report and assumed that he had already read it and had no questions about it.

This form of manipulation may also seem a little dishonest but it is a common practice in corporate offices. How do you think that many of these corporations are getting away with millions if not billions of dollars from legal contracts that keep the average customer from figuring out. One telecommunications company has a contract they give to their customers for a simple monthly phone service that is sixty pages long. Don't think you're the first one to try this and don't expect that others are going to let opportunities slip through their fingers by not doing the same.

**Create an Illusion of Choice:** When you want to be sure that your boss will make a decision in your favor, you can create an illusion that makes him think he has a choice.

Start by preparing three possible methods for dealing with a specific situation. However, you want to be sure that at two of the options you give him only seem like possibilities but if actually put into force would prove to be non-starters. You might offer an option that puts his bonus in jeopardy, or you might present an option that everyone on the team would object to. The third option would be the one you actually want him to make. Your boss will usually consider all three options and then make his choice.

While this is a very effective approach, your boss will likely appreciate your hard work in doing such thorough research in helping him, you need to exercise this strategy with caution. You can't make what you're doing too obvious. If your two additional options are not believable or within the realm of possibilities, your boss will figure out what you're doing and it could end up causing you more harm than good.

Wording is key in this arena. By phrasing the two options that are not viable with words like "courageous" or "bold" it will give him the idea that you think he's strong enough to handle such a bold decision but will cause him to feel more cautious in his approach. The trick to success is in carefully creating seemingly viable bad choices that seem equal in nature to the one you want him to make.

**Overworked:** This one works well when you want to get out of doing assignments you don't really like. Start by adjusting your appearance. When you're in the office, make it a point to walk around with a large stack of papers in your arms. As a habit, walk fast and give the appearance that you're always on your way to do something, even if it's just a trip to the bathroom.

If he asks you how you're doing, answer with a roll of the eyes and a quick answer. "I'm frazzled," "I don't know how I manage to muster up enough energy to do this or that." "I'm muddling my way through it." If your office has additional meetings to sign up for, try to get in as many as you can so that you can honestly say you're too busy. Your goal is to give the appearance that you're just too busy to take on any additional work.

What usually happens is that you'll develop a reputation for always working hard and you'll gain the sympathy vote. Your boss will see this and as he hears comments from others about your diligence at your job, he'll be reluctant to add any more to your workload and give additional work to someone else in the office.

This is a very effective strategy but it will only work with the kind of boss who values hard work over measurable results. If you have the kind of boss that wants actual reports and solid proof of what you're doing, this is not going to be the best approach.

**Wrong place at the wrong time:** This is a deliberate strategy that puts you in the wrong place at the wrong time. Your goal is to make it inconvenient for your boss to respond as he usually would to your suggestions. You might pitch an idea at a time when he's in a meeting with a client or on the phone under the guise of being helpful.

Just before the meeting begins give him a large stack of information to throw him off balance. You could also make an expression just before he's ready to launch into his spiel. As you hand him the information add a phrase like, "I just heard that he didn't like the last presentation someone gave him, so it's up to you to kill it in there. Here, I thought this information would help."

The message will be so unnerving to him that he will lose his focus. He will go in the meeting but his inability to concentrate will cause him to fumble or make a major mistake as a result.

Here there are two things that are important to happen at the right time. First, your timing has to be exactly right. Too soon and you give him a chance to recover, too late and you miss your window. Second, your message has to be vague enough that he won't have any way to verify it.

Other than that, you need to make sure that he understands you're not trying to undermine his work, but that you only want to be helpful.

## Killer Negotiation Strategies to Manipulate Your Way to Success

The art of negotiation is one area of business where manipulation can prove to be very powerful. If fact, it is the one place where manipulation is not only effective but also necessary. Whether you're buying a new car or you're closing a major multi-million dollar deal on a prime piece of real estate, learning the psychology behind manipulation and negotiation practices can save you a massive amount of money, time, and energy.

**Disappointment:** Letting the other person see disappointment in you can be very effective. Studies have shown that just the appearance of disappointment is all that is needed to boost the size of your concessions made in your favor. If you're considering a new car for example, you might notice the salesman appear like he isn't pleased with your offer. There is a method to his madness. He may be very happy with your offer but acting disappointed makes you feel guilty and compels you to offer more or opens the door for him to ask for more. It also lowers the chance of you changing your mind and having second thoughts about lowering your offer.

When this is done on the first offer, it puts you in the power position in the negotiation process. Since power people rarely accept the first offer given, the direction the offers move will be based on how you respond. Fake disappointment lets you decide which way the next offer will go.

**The Anti-Negotiation Buster:** When the other party plays the disappointment card on you, how you respond could put the ball back in your court. By responding with a statement like, "I'm sorry, I don't have the authority to respond to such a good offer, I'll have to defer to my superiors." They will usually respond with a number they want, and the ball is back in your court again.

**"You can do better than that":** Silence is a great tool for any negotiator. We are psychologically hard-wired to fill in the blanks when there is too much lag time between conversations. That's why when bill collectors call, they usually will say something like we haven't received your bill for this month," and then they will remain quiet.

The don't push or ask what happened, and almost always you will feel the pressure of the silence to say something. That's when you start to make excuses or explain why you haven't paid your bill.

This same tactic works well in negotiations. When you tell them that they have to do better and then wait, more often than not, they will make the concession. Silence makes you the master of the negotiation.

**The Defensive Strategy:** This strategy uses reverse psychology as its foundation. Manipulators use this when they are dealing with a person, they haven't been able to gain their trust or when other forms of manipulation haven't worked yet.

By telling them that they are "being defensive" and then follow it immediately with a joke at their expense, it takes much of the stress out of the situation. Think how you would react to a statement like this in the middle of a negotiation.

"My goodness don't be so defensive. Just relax a little, we're just discussing a great deal for you. If you accept it, you'll bankrupt us unless we can get you to put down your defensive walls se we can get something out of it too."

The statement is designed to get the other person to lower his guard and maybe even laugh a little. It also gets him to think that the negotiations are already going in his favor and he may lose the deal if he doesn't start making even more concessions.

If someone uses this tactic on you, how would you respond? In most cases, one might find himself compelled to let down his guard in an effort to prove him wrong. Don't fall for this trick. The best response would be to say something like, "The way you are pushing this deal is what is making me defensive. If you want me to take this a little further, this is why…."

This kind of defense puts you back in the driver's seat and you have control once again of the negotiations. You could also make a joke. "Don't take it so seriously. We're all friends here, if things don't go your way, you could always come over to my place. You do cook, don't you?"

**Getting to the higher authority:** In most cases, when a person says they have some freedom in deciding a price, you can pretty much bet that they won't have the final say on anything. In fact, it means that they don't have much power at all. You need to find the person who is really in charge of what happens in the negotiations. This is usually someone who is just pretending to be a small fry.

They may be the silent one at the table who is pretending like he has no control at all over the situation. They do this so they can use the "fly on the wall" strategy to find out information and play all sorts of games with you.

By presenting yourself as a fake higher authority, you can successfully:

- Delay the negotiations until a time when you're better prepared.

- Take a stronger stance without looking like the bad guy.
- Offer a last minute concession if necessary.

There are several ways to respond when someone uses this negotiation strategy on you:

- Go along with it but make a mental note of the game he's playing. You could respond by saying, "You're not going to play the good cop/bad cop game on me, are you?"
- You could agree and then tell them, "when you do meet with your boss let him know I'd like to meet him."
- Or you could call him on it and tell him you now he's the boss.

**Last Minute Approval:** On nearly every occasion if someone is pushing for a last-minute concession, you know you're dealing with a master manipulator. There are many ways, they can show their hand. They may agree to the transaction and then inform you that they need an additional approval from someone else. They will give the appearance that the agreement is done but then hold back on finalizing everything. Later, they will come back and tell you that their boss is being very difficult.

If this happens to you, when they return, tell them that you also have a higher authority and you need to defer to them for a final decision. When you return, ask for your own concession. If they need the deal more than you do, this could turn into a final showdown. You could put yourself into a position where you could easily blindside them with a little pressure.

For example, "Listen, I gave this some serious consideration and I really want to hold my position here. I don't like going against my word, but I think I need to ask for 10% more." Then later, you could feel guilty about it and then make a small concession. "Because I quoted you a different price before, I can give you a 5% break, but I need an answer soon. Can you get back to me by the end of the week?"

**Good Cop/Bad Cop:** This is an expression that all of us know and we usually associate it with legal authorities, but it works well if you have a partner at the negotiation table too. In each case, the bad cop is the one who is firm in his position and doesn't want to budge. When too much demand is on the table the bad cop feigns anger and storms out of the room leaving the good cop to play the nice guy. The good cop then plays the higher authority card and defers to the bad cop for the final decision.

If someone plays this game on you, don't be afraid to present your own bad cop. If that doesn't work, pretend like you're giving in and use what they do next to your advantage. For example, if the good cop presents an offer you then know what they consider a good deal and what they want, but you also know what you won't accept.

## Fractionation: The Seduction Tool of Master Manipulators

Have you ever wondered why "that guy" was the one to always get the girl? Why he or she seemed to always have someone hanging off of their arm, but you never seemed to be able to get past first base with anyone? No matter who you are or where you're from, there always seems to be someone who is able to do what you felt was close to be the impossible when it comes to relationships.

In order to have a close relationship with anyone, you need to be able to draw people to you. The common belief was that attracting people was a matter of looks, mannerisms, and sex appeal. However, now according to studies in modern psychology, attraction appears to be well within the reach of anyone and everyone through developing the manipulative skill of fractionation.

The name is derived from its basic scientific definition: *a separation process in which one mixture is divided into a number of smaller parts.* This seems an unusual term to use when trying to attract the opposite sex, which most of us would agree needs some level of skill in the art of seduction, but if you stick with me here, you will see how it fits.

When it comes to relationships, fractionation combines several theories all into one. With the careful use of psychology, persuasion, and the mysterious art of hypnosis, you can attract almost anyone to you. Basically, when you boil it down to the basics, it is simply the manipulative side of seduction. Because of its power to attract, many will question whether it is right or wrong to use it. However, the decision of if or how you use it is entirely up to you. Many claim that you can attract another person in as little as 15 minutes.

With all the hype surrounding fractionation, it almost sounds scary and mystical as if it were a part of the dark arts. In reality though, it could just as easily be described as a conversation technique designed with the sole purpose of bringing out strong emotions in the other person. Emotions so strong that will automatically connect them to you.

***The Preparation:*** If attracting someone of the opposite sex were as easy as just walking up and talking to them then everyone would have someone by their side. In order to effectively use this strategy, you need to dedicate some time to preparation. Before you begin, there are certain skills you should work on developing:

- Leadership skills: Especially if you are a man, most women are not interested in a follower. If you are a woman, most men are interested in an independent woman but not an overbearing one. Learn to be more balanced and flexible.
- Your uniqueness: You don't want to appear as someone that just fell out of a mold. You need an interest that will ensure that you stand out from the crowd.
- Social skills: Build up your confidence in speaking with the opposite sex while in a crowd. Practice talking to both men and women in different settings until you are able to

- comfortably develop a casual conversation no matter where you are.
- Know the playing field: Learn about all the hot spots where people you're interested in like to gather. Be familiar with various options so when these places come up in discussion, you can easily participate. It also gives you a few great places to recommend if you want to invite someone out.

All of these qualities can only be done if you approach every encounter with confidence. Note, the word used is confidence, not arrogance. Statistics show that confidence is the most attractive quality to people. If you seriously want to attract someone into your life, get rid of your awkward shyness and let to present yourself in a more positive light.

Your goal with this type of preparation is to position yourself so that you will look desirable in the other person's eyes. Note, all of these things should be done before you open your mouth and say your very first word.

Make it a habit to always look your best every time you walk out your door. Spruce up your wardrobe so you have something trendy and appealing. While looks don't account for everything when it comes to attracting the opposite sex, it does matter. No one wants someone unkempt and slovenly on their arm. This doesn't mean you have to wear the most expensive clothes or the latest styles, but at the very least, make sure the clothes you wear are or were stylish within the last decade and are net and clean.

***Your Emotions:*** The art of fractionation is very similar to the style of writing used in those addictive soap operas watched every day. Ask yourself, why are people glued to the TV set to watch a fictitious story come to life. It's because it is easy, the characters are those they can relate to and the story line taps into their **emotions.** This works because at the core of seduction is always emotion. There can be no seduction if emotions are not involved. This means more than saying pretty words, you're evoking a form of mind control so you'll need to pull out all the weapons in your arsenal including using your body language, controlling your tone of voice, and even some subtle forms of hypnosis.

As you choose your target, don't let your own insecurities get in the way. Never downplay the value of what you have to offer to a relationship. That means, the general idea that "she's out of my league," should not be part of the thought process. Instead, you want them to think they are not in your field, but you want them to feel confident enough that they can reach for it. This creates an area of challenge that will have them believing that you are worthy of the chase.

When you have carefully chosen your target, you are ready to employ your skills in fractionation. Begin with your conversational style. This is where you will apply your excellent conversational skills. Remember, conversation is more than just spewing out the right words but you need to learn to speak with your body as well. Your aim is to not to create a physical attraction but to establish a relationship. Your new relationship should be built on trust, which will be vital if you ever hope the relationship to last more than just a few days. This will require having to ask a lot of questions in order to get her involved in the conversation but be careful. It is not a job interview, just enough questions to show that you are interested, but not enough to make them feel like you're prying, nosey, or a busybody.

Conversation should be compelling and emotionally diverse. What I mean by that is that it should never display one emotion, you want to stir up a range of feelings. Your goal is to build up the kind of conversation they would want to be a part of. Choose topics that will have the emotional ups and downs and use them as an anchor to hold them in. From there you can pivot in any direction you want and they will follow.

Getting started is the tricky part. Start by asking probing but non-invasive questions to get the conversation started. You could ask them to tell you about something that makes them happy. Or you could ask her about something relating to another powerful emotion. After skillfully doing that they will happily follow you through a whole barrage of conversational topics. By tapping into both positive and negative emotions one right after the other and employing your other conversational skills like voice inflections, tone, and body language, you've hooked them in.

So, how do you choose a topic that is going to be the initial draw and then keep it moving forward. Think polarity or focus on alternating with a sequence of opposite emotions. Pleasure/pain/pleasure/pain and so on. The longer you can keep this string going the stronger the bond you will build.

For example, "Have you ever been very close to someone. So close that you felt like you were two sides of the same person and then suddenly they were gone? They just died?" This sentence starts off with something full of joy and happiness and then ends with an emotional downturn of loss and sadness.

Another example: "Have you ever met someone and was sure that they were the one for you? That the two of you were destined to stay together? And then suddenly they left? Something happened to break you apart?"

As you can see from the above examples, your questions have to have some level of depth to them. Don't settle for the superficial expressions commonly heard. Look for ways to introduce topics that will be intriguing and get them to express their innermost feelings.

It's not always easy to find ways to weave these types of questions into a regular conversation and it will take practice. However, once you do, you have started a new relationship with someone that you can now start to build on over time. Fractionation can be a challenge but eventually you will be able to master it and as a result, make yourself more attractive and interesting to others.

The whole idea behind fractionation is to create an aura of suspense. Think soap operas. Don't charge in right away with statements like you're really into them. These rarely work because you can't be interested in someone you know nothing about. It only tells them that you want to get them into bed. People want a challenge they can work for so make don't make it too easy to gain your interest. If they feel too comfortable, they will quickly lose interest and move on to someone else.

Confusion can also be very effective in attracting others. If you're very interested one minute and nonchalant the next it creates a question in their mind. They'll want to get to know you better to find out what's really under the surface.

***What to avoid:*** This is only the beginning of a relationship. As time passes, you will have to continue to find new ways to keep interest. As you build on the foundation you've laid, try to avoid the following:

- Using bad manners: we live in a world where manners have been thrown out the window but that should not be your excuse. Always fall back on courtesy and respect.
- Talking about your exes: no matter how much you've been hurt or disappointed in the past, it should never be part of a conversation with a new relationship.
- Downplaying their emotions: An angry person never likes being told to calm down. While you may not agree with how they feel, their emotions are real and valid to them.
- Posting pictures with other women or men

You get the picture. Remember, you are trying to draw them to you. Men complaining about women's monthly period or her mood swings is just going to put a damper on all your hard work. By the same token, women who challenge his masculinity will rarely be a basis for a long-standing relationship.

There is no question that starting a new relationship is difficult. The combination of nerves and emotions can be hard to cope with. However, if you feel you're ready to embark on this adventure, it is not impossible. Build up your confidence and give it your best shot. If once you've started, you don't feel comfortable in the new relationship, don't be afraid to walk away. It is much better than dragging out a bad match to spare their feelings. It will only hurt more later on.

## 11 Less-Known Manipulation Techniques for Seduction

Going just a step further, after you've drawn the person in, your next goal is to keep them there until they are just as committed to you as you are to them. This is not always easy, but if you've kept your EQ high, it can be easier than you think.

There are a lot of ways to keep someone by your side but if you want to employ tools that will make the **want** to be by your side, then you should pay close attention to the patterns of their behavior. Observe what they do when they are just being themselves and use these as cues as to what you can do to keep them interested. Depending on your observations you can use any one or a combination of the following manipulation techniques to advance your relationship to the next level.

**Flattery:** Flattery is different from giving a regular or a genuine compliment to someone. It is actually giving compliments that are not necessary. Be careful when you flatter someone; it can have dangerous repercussions. By flattering someone so as to fuel their own insecurities, they may be drawn to you or they may start to view you suspiciously. A good example of this is if you flatter a man who is not very confident in his own sense of masculinity, he may enjoy hearing your words of praise but he may be equally suspicious about the sincerity of your words. Ideally, you want to find out what makes them insecure and give them just enough support to bolster their confidence but not go overboard.

Ex: "You're such a tough guy, you intimidate everyone around you." This will flatter a man with who is insecure about his masculinity.

Ex: "You're my little baby doll." This will flatter a woman who may be insecure about her weight.

**The Trojan Horse:** Some might describe this tactic as a bribe. If you keep showering them with gifts, no matter how small, they will feel obligated to stay with you. This can be done very subtly as in the case of buying a meal. This will make them feel obligated to have regular conversation with you but some have actually gone to extremes. For example, some have paid to support the other's entire lifestyle, putting them in homes, giving them cars, etc. In such cases, the extent of indebtedness grows. In those instances, they may feel as if they own the other person, which carries with it its own set of risks.

**The Silent Treatment:** The absence of communication can have earth shattering effects when they have become accustomed to regular conversation. This type of manipulation can easily unnerve a person and make them feel they have done something wrong and they will go out of their way to fix it for you.

**The Mirror:** People have also put on pretenses in order to keep someone with them. They may pretend to share the same values or demonstrate that they like the same things. Manipulators have even been known to fabricate a completely new story line in order to attract others. The sole purpose of the mirror is to give the other person exactly what they need to hear to boost their emotional stability.

**Make the Decision for Them:** Man are usually the ones to take this tactic. In an effort to assert their masculinity, they may make decisions for the other person. By deciding what they will eat, where they will go, or what they will do, the other person over time will become dependent on them and they won't want to leave.

**The Big Question:** This involves asking them for something that is far more than you know they can afford to give. You know they will be forced to refuse but, in an attempt, to compromise, they will settle for the very thing you want from them in the first place. For example, you can ask them to move in with you, which you know it is too early in the relationship for that. Then you can ask for something that is less risky, like going away for a weekend together.

**The Logical Fallacy:** Planting the idea in their mind that if they don't do what you want then they don't have feelings for you or they don't love you. Teenagers often use this manipulation tactic quite effectively. "If you loved me you would do this or do that."

**The Expected:** You might attempt to keep them by telling them it is only normal that you do this or that. "We've been together for six months now. It's only logical that we start living together."

**The Guilt Trip:** There are often attempts to make the other person feel ashamed for not continuing with the relationship. By making them feel like they have taken advantage of you, they will feel guilty for their own behavior and will stick with you. This tactic only works when you know the other person well and you know exactly which buttons to push, but when used properly, it can be very effective.

**The Remote Control:** Every time the other person starts to talk about leaving change the subject to something you know they are keenly interested in. They won't be able to resist switching with you and the fated conversation will be put off to another day.

**The Board Game:** When they ask to do something you don't want to do, you can also shame them by questioning their motives. "Is that what you really want?" Done the right way, it can make the other person feel like they were being unreasonable for even bringing the subject up.

Keep in mind that these tactics will only work for you temporarily. There are few manipulation strategies that will keep the other person connected to do indefinitely if there is not a genuine and compatible match. So, while manipulation may have its place in a new relationship, in time, you will eventually have to work on building that relationship on honest conversation and a real emotional connection between the two of you.

**Love Bombing:** The art of "love bombing" does not necessarily apply exclusively to romantic relationships. In fact, it's origin started in a church setting where religious leaders developed it to attract new parishioners to their pews. They literally "bombed" them with lots of attention and affection. Over time, parents started using it as an innovative way to education their children through kindness and care. Over time, others grew to see that it could be a powerful tool that can be used to control people in all sorts of settings. Whether it's through the use of kind words, the warmth of a tender embrace, or through the corny actions the success was impressive as more and more people started being drawn into people they would never have given a second look at before.

The basis of love bombing is to display your target with lots of affection and attention in an effort to show that you are the partner of their dreams. Once they are convinced that you are a hopeless romantic and your target is convinced that you are the ideal partner for them they are ready to enter into what they expect to be an ideal relationship.

For this strategy to work, it must be done in several stages. In the initial stage, everything must be flawless in every way. This would involve performing acts specifically designed to gain their trust, giving them encouraging words to build them up emotionally, and giving them the needed support and patience when needed.

Over time, these acts can pull a person closer to you until the point when you are able to emotionally dominate them. Evil manipulators will slowly begin to extend that control and keep them tied to them through a barrage of text messages and phone calls when they're not together. By the time this begins to happen, the other person is so hopelessly dedicated that even if they do detect something is not right, their own insecurities will be so powerful that they will find it hard to break it off. They have become addicted to those large doses of praise and kindness. That's the point when a manipulator can start to take advantage of the situation.

This is an extreme form of manipulation and those who usually practice it are generally those who have a very low self-esteem to begin with. They only use love bombing because they don't believe that they can seduce a person all on their own. They feel the only way they can have a relationship is by trickery, lies, and mind control. They recognize if they have complete dominance over the other person there is no way they will ever be abandoned.

The cycle of love bombing is difficult to miss. It can be easily identified if you know what you're looking for. The resulting relationship is not based on any form of true connection but is mostly founded on the idea of a romantic relationship. The concept of "soulmates" is at the heart and the person begins to believe that everything is so perfect that it must've been fate that brought you together. Once the target accepts this belief, the relationship can quickly turn toxic.

In the beginning, everything seems like a dream come true to the victim as the manipulator dazzles them with a chaotic array of attention and affection. The onslaught of romantic words and phrases are so frequent and steady that the victim may come to believe it so strongly that they are blinded to many of the faults even when they are played out right in front of their eyes. Once it reaches this point, it is nearly impossible for the victim to break free from the hold they manipulator has on them.

There are several phases of love bombing:

***Devaluation:*** This stage happens after the initial phase of compliments, affection, and lots of attention. In the devaluation phase, the manipulator turns that attention to disapproval and anger. This easily can escalate into threats, which is a huge part of the psychological conditional that allows them to become a dictator of the other person's behavior.

These first two cycles could repeat themselves over and over again until it reaches a major climax.

***Letting go:*** After the relationship has escalated into abuse, victims begin to ignore their own needs just so they can stay attached to the manipulator. Given enough time, they will break away from family and friends, and give up all the things they once loved just in an effort to avoid or break away from the conflicts that may arise.

Sometimes it can take an intervention to help the victim separate themselves from the relationship. If the person has some level of emotional strength, they may find a way to break it off on their own. They may grow tired of being controlled or they may just be feeling the pressure from others to help them to break free.

If you're truly looking for a lasting relationship, you want to avoid trying the love bomb strategy. While it may draw a person to you, it won't ever be for the reasons you want. If you suspect someone is love bombing you, use your senses. They may shower you with compliments and gifts, even if you don't know them very well. They may give you a classic line like "I know we're just made for each other."

They also know how to identify someone who would be susceptible to their witty charms. They may openly talk about a past relationship on the first date. They may lament about how the other person didn't appreciate them or how they felt misunderstood, detailing all the elements of their breakup. When that happens, beware. They are trying to pull you in and play the sympathy card. Their words are carefully chosen so that you will listen to them and feel their pain.

Once they can convince you of their "feelings" it is just a matter of time before they start to control you.

Breaking up from a love bomber is difficult but it can be done. However, they will continue to ply you with affections in an effort to win you back. If you want to keep separate from them there is only one way to do this. You must break all ties with them and avoid any contact whatsoever. You also need to get support so pool together those who you trust to help you resist the temptation to go back. And no matter what you do, don't blame yourself for falling for this highly effective trick. Just be happy you were able to break free and move on from there.

# Chapter Seven: Advanced Manipulation Tactics

Psychological manipulation can be very subtle and it can be quite obtuse. Depending on your aim, you will decide which tactics will work best to get you what you need. Up until this point, the manipulation strategies we have discussed have been pretty simple and basic. A lot of these things can easily be picked up on your own simply by observing the interactions of the world around you. However, when these other more basic methods fail to work, there are several advanced methods you can try.

The Manipulative Power of Reinforcement

One key element of manipulation is the art of reinforcement. It's a form of behavioral psychology that allows the user to help mold his target's future behavior by giving them some form of reinforcement. By applying this strategy, you can gain a measure of control over your subject and by extension mold his conduct himself in ways that you want to see.

There are two types of reinforcement that can be applied. Positive reinforcement is the kind of stimulus that will encourage them to continue conducting themselves in a way that you approve of. Negative reinforcement would give stimulus that has been chosen to change their behavior to something else.

Of course, there are many different degrees to the type of stimulus you can provide depending on the type of results you seek. If you want them to perform the behavior more frequently or to continue the behavior for a longer period of time then you would use positive reinforcement. If you're looking for them to change their behavior or to lessen the frequency of the behavior you would use negative reinforcement. Depending on the type of reinforcement you use, you can get a wide range of results.

***Rewarding Stimuli:*** The stimuli you use as a reinforcement must be chosen very carefully. If you hope it can be at all effective, you need to understand what your subject wants and likes. The reward has to tap into their basic needs for desire and pleasure or their use will be ineffective. We all have basic needs that drive us to do the things we do so when your reward taps into that inner need, it is more likely to encourage more of the behavior you want. In essence, reinforcement happens only if the subject sees the stimuli as a reward or in the case of negative reinforcement, as a loss.

Parents are very effective at using reinforcement to get their children to do their chores. They may offer an allowance for doing work around the house or they may offer a weekend at an amusement park for exceptionally good behavior. But when you look around you, we see the art of reinforcement playing out in every field. Few of us go to work just because we enjoy the work and it makes us feel good. We go for the paycheck/reward. Few of us are in relationships where we're not getting some form of satisfaction out of it. And we rarely spend our free time doing things we hate. When we get a moment free to ourselves, we naturally go for the things that we feel are most rewarding to us. Getting a raise or a promotion at work is a powerful incentive for getting you to work harder on your job. By the same token, losing your job for undesirable behavior can be a strong negative reinforcement as well.

In most situations, the use of reinforcement is relating to behavior but it can also relate to memory as well. A good example of this is something called "post-training reinforcement" where the reward is given after the subject has learned something new. A manipulator can use reinforcement to help improve their memory of the breadth, duration, and specific details of the lesson until it is firmly planted in their mind. In such cases, the reward needs to be something that touches the subject emotionally. That way, they connect the lesson with their personal feelings.

We've all experienced this type of reward before. If you are of the older generation, you can recall without much hesitation where you were when the Challenger exploded or the 9/11 tragedy occurred. These have been described as "flashbulb memories" because they were both events that give us intense emotions. If you look back through your own personal life, those memories that are the embedded the deepest in your mind are the very ones that have touched you emotionally. This can be an extremely powerful emotional tool when used in the right way.

In order to use reinforcement successfully, you will need to fully understand where your target is vulnerable. This information will help you to decide which type of reward you will give them in order to mold their behavior. Once decided, you must be careful not to be too over when giving the reward. When it is too obvious, the subject is very likely to understand what's going on and squash your efforts almost immediately. However, by playing a subtle and more passive role, you can gently nudge them in the direction you want them to go.

***Applying Positive Reinforcement:*** One of the easiest forms of reinforcement is when you encourage continued practice of a desirable behavior. Your reward will be given as a means of encouraging the subject to continue or to escalate a certain act. Some examples of positive reinforcement:
- You can give words of praise encouraging them to continue.
- Money
- Approval
- Gifts
- Personal attention

- Public recognition

Positive reinforcement does not have to cost you anything. Small children for example are happy with just an approving smile from their parents. Don't get into the habit of thinking that positive reinforcement has to have a monetary value. Look for what that person needs and use that to encourage them. Even adults are not always content with monetary value. People see value in all sorts of things.

***Applying Negative Reinforcement:*** When you want your subject to cut back or cease a certain behavior then you would apply negative reinforcement. In such a case, you would remove a reward or you would prevent them from achieving the reward they seek. Negative reinforcement could also include giving them something they don't find desirable; something that will either make them uncomfortable or find to be unpleasant. Such reinforcement is less likely to keep them continuing with the same behavior for any extended period of time.
- Nagging
- Intimidation
- Yelling
- Swearing
- Guilt trip
- Silent treatment
- Sulking

You will notice that all of the behaviors listed above can make your subject extremely uncomfortable. They play on his emotions and erode their personal self-esteem causing them to cease their behavior. Consider what happens when a parent nags their child about doing house chores. If every time the child enters the room, the parent nags, yells, screams, embarrasses, or threatens the child will eventually start doing his chores. The reward happens when the chores are done and the parent stops berating them.

Another example, an employer has a policy that all work must be completed by the end of the week or they can't have the weekend off. This is a powerful negative reinforcer and gives many workers incentive to increase their productivity during the week so that everything will be done on time.

***Extinction:*** Reinforcement can also take a neutral position too. Positive reinforcers are used to encourage the behavior you want, negative reinforcers are designed to discourage certain behaviors. Extinction reinforcers, however, happens when you don't acknowledge the behavior at all.

For example, a child refusing to acknowledge a bully at school. With neither a positive or a negative reaction, there is no fuel for the bully to work with and he will quickly lose interest in his target. It can also be seen when employers do not recognize the work that an employee is doing. In time, the employee will lose interest in his work and will give up trying.

Keep in mind that reinforcement is not the same as punishment. Punishment is designed to correct certain behaviors and reinforcement is designed to encourage behaviors. You could think of them as the opposites of the same coin.

## Charming Habits to Manipulate Anyone

Charisma can be an excellent tool for manipulating anyone. When you can be charming you are also endearing to others and they will be drawn to you. However, there is a big difference between being charming and acting charming. Some people just have a natural way of pulling people in while others may have to work at it. It's not as easy as they make it appear to be.

When you can put on the charm, it is easy to blind someone to your true intentions. By nature, people tend to listen to only those things they want to hear. They often make decisions that they know are against their best interest yet they do it anyway without giving it a second thought.

There are those who already know how to use their charm to draw us in, giving us a strong sense of confidence. Others use their charm to get you to let your guard down so you will believe everything they say. And others will use their charm to make you feel like you've been friends for years even when you've only just met. All of these people are highly skilled at turning it on and off at will making it very difficult to recognize it when it's being put to use. If you're not one of these people you will have to develop these skills that are classics for master manipulators.

*Mirroring:* Mirroring or matching the other person's body language sends them a signal letting them know that you are very interested in them. It builds a bond of trust that you can use later on when you want to get something from them or get them to do something for you.

In a normal setting, people will automatically do this without even realizing it. However, it can be one of the most effective ways to win someone over when you are using it to connect with the other person. Think of how many times you've smiled when you caught someone mirroring you. Perhaps you both reached for the same book at the same time. Your hands touch and you can't help but smile when you realize what happens. On a subconscious level, you are letting the person know that you have more in common than they may have realized.

***Gazing Into Their Eyes:*** We all know how important making eye contact is when trying to communicate. It is one of the best ways to get people feel like they matter to you. When using this technique when you are trying to persuade someone you can lock your eyes with theirs with an intense gaze that can seem almost hypnotic. For the best effect, timing is important.

For example, locking eyes with them immediately after saying something that might may them feel uneasy can temper the kind of response they give you. It throws them off their game and disorients them for a minute. That will give your initial thought time to sink in.

***Breaking the Rules:*** There is a reason why the bad guy always seems to get the girl. There is a certain charm quality they all seem to have. They may be breaking the rules but they are doing it in a playful way. They are not breaking the rules just to break them though; there is a method to their madness. They may try some intimate moves with you on the first date. Touching you in a way you would not normally permit.

This kind of behavior is really a fishing expedition. They are pushing the boundaries so they can see where you stand. How committed are you to your decisions. How you respond to these tests will determine the method of manipulation to use in the future. If you permit intimate touching on the first date, you can fully expect the intimacy to escalate in the future.

As a general rule, manipulators will use these charming qualities to invade your space, draw your attention, and to show their power over their target. Think of it as playing a game of chess where they are making a play for control over the subject's mind and heart.

***Confessions:*** One thing charming people know how to do is talk. They are very eloquent speakers and know how to pull you into a conversation and hold your attention until they have made their point. They are avid attention seekers and to do this they need to know how to tell a story that will keep you hanging on every word.

Manipulators will do the same thing on a more personal level. Rather than telling a good story they will tell you about confidential matters to keep you coming back. They make you feel as if they trust you so much, they will share their innermost secrets with you. This is usually the first part of a manipulation strategy. They start by getting you to connect with them by confessing all their past deeds. They will continue until you are so involved you look for them to tell you more. Then they stop, literally pulling the rug right from under your feet, refusing to even discuss such things anymore. This leaves you feeling like you've done something wrong and you will do just about anything to get back to that same level of communication you had before.

***Using Pet Names:*** On the surface, calling your significant other by pet names seems endearing and affectionate, but in reality, it is devaluing your role in the relationship. Calling someone baby, or sweetie, or darling shows that they are not seeing you as an equal in the relationship. It makes you feel lesser than you really are.

If they continue this habit for a long time and then stop, you begin to feel as if you're in the wrong and wondering what to do about it. At that point, they have maneuvered you into a position where they now have control over you and you will become their puppet and do exactly what they want just to hear those endearing words again.

***Excessive Complimenting:*** Sometimes excessive complimenting is truly sincere but this tool in the hands of a master manipulator can be covering over questionable motives. This form of manipulation is usually done by those who are lower on the totem pole than others within the infrastructure. Children will do this to their parents, employees to their bosses, and students to teachers.

Be cautious when using this technique, most people in positions of power will be on guard so you will have to exercise a little self-control and use it gradually over a longer period of time. If you can effectively do this subtly then your chances of getting a harder more difficult person to soften up will be a lot easier than if you go in guns a blazing and gushing all over them.

***Validating Negative Emotions:*** Helping people justify negative emotions is a powerful weapon in the hands of a manipulator. If they are feeling depressed about a mistake or something they feel they did wrong, rather than encourage you to change, a manipulator will validate those feelings so that you will stay in a negative frame of mind. Then when they have you fully committed to them, they will be your redeemer and rescue you.

This type of manipulator is not interested in making you feel better but wants you to believe that they are the solution to all your problems. They want you to believe that you cannot resolve the issue on your own so they will try to keep you trapped in that negative emotional state so they can rescue you.

It may take some time to develop these skills to a degree where you can turn them on and off without much though however, once you do, you will have all the charm and grace that you see so many others engaged in.

How to Turn Someone Into their Own Enemy
Our memories are a tricky thing. We often question whether we remember events accurately anyway, so it can be relatively easy for a

manipulator to play on that natural tendency to turn someone's own recollections against them. This method of persuasion is called "gaslighting" and it is used to get someone to trust you more than they do themselves.

You can see gaslighting going on all around you. It is used by lawyers, relationship partners, religious leaders, and other with the sole purpose of making the other person believe that their memories or recollection of events is fallible. When you can convince someone that there is something wrong with how the recall events it erodes their confidence in themselves so you can then implant in them your own script for them to play out.

*Addiction:* It is one thing to call a person crazy and it is another thing entirely to convince them of it. They are not likely to believe you just because you said it so, you will need to start doing things to convince them of your truth. Before you can do that, you have to get them to trust you.

This starts with triggering the brain to release endorphins and dopamine. When a person gets excited a chemical reaction starts in the brain and it releases those hormones. These are the same hormones that are released when people take drugs. By doing things to trigger the same chemical release, you can cause a person to become addicted to you. Your first step in gaslighting is to create an addict by providing them with enough excitement that they will attach themselves to you just so they can continue to get that high from the chemical release in their brains.

*Work on Your Own Memory:* Now you have to work on yourself. It is a given that we all make mistakes but that doesn't mean that we remember them all. An effective manipulator is very meticulous and will remember every time a mistake is made by their subject and any misinterpretations or misunderstandings they may have developed.

You need this so that you can use this as evidence that their memories are not legitimate and not to be relied upon.

By frequently pointing these normal flaws out, your subject will eventually begin to see how frequently they are in the wrong and will start to rely on your memory and solutions when problems come up.

*Act Confused:* When your subject raises an objection to your representation of the facts, you can act confused and feign a lack of understanding. Or you can dismiss his recounting as exaggerated, illogical, or completely false. Then you can present your own answer as a simple but logical account of the events. After doing this several times, the subject will start to turn to you for help more and more as they lose their own confidence in their abilities.

*Forget:* When they tell you they did this or that, simply tell them you don't recall it. Use phrases like, "I don't remember that," or "I didn't see you there." Be persistent even when it comes to the smallest detail. The more insistent you are the less likely they are going to resist your influence.

You could also do the opposite and convince someone that they really did do something you know they didn't do. This will confuse them even more because they will struggle to recall events that never happened. Again, if you project confidence and persistence in your belief they will begin to doubt their own memory and eventually fall in line with your thinking.

*Minimize Their Concerns:* Over time, gaslighting will drain your subjects to the point of frustration and depression. It will bring out a lot of negative emotions, which can be thoroughly exhausting. Once that happens, they will begin to talk about their concerns and they will turn to you because 1) they're now addicted to you. 2) they lack confidence in their own memory, and 3) you have positioned yourself to be a trustworthy ally. When they come to you with their concerns, dismiss them by telling them that they are "taking things too seriously," "overreacting, or getting too emotional.

This can turn out to be one of the most effective manipulation tools you can have in your arsenal. The best and most efficient way to use it is slowly over an extended period of time. You may not be able to master it correctly the first time, but after several tries, you will be able to turn someone's mind into his own enemy. Then you have them in a position to do whatever you want from them.

# Chapter Eight: Asserting Dominance

It is relatively easy to see the kind of people that are drawn to us. We tend to gravitate towards those who are similar to us in behavior and thought. There is a lot of truth in the old saying "birds of a feather flock together." We surround ourselves with people who are going to relate to us, understand us, and support us. It saves us from constantly having to live with a defensive stance over all of our decisions.

However, as a manipulator, you will want someone around you that will behave in a certain way so you will need to exercise some level of control. You will have to assert your dominance from the very beginning so that they will follow your every instruction without question. You not only want to be able to direct their behavior but you want them to accept it too. For this you need to develop some very strong skills.

## Body Language that Asserts Dominance

Your body is your largest form of communication. How you move or position it will cause others to react without question. One of the reasons to exercise dominance with your body is because it is subtle, almost invisible, so it is unlikely the other person will even realize what you're doing. We react to body language instinctively, without thought, so once they respond to you, their thoughts will naturally fall in line.

*Use of Space:* When people are being described as being "larger than life" it's not referring to their physical size, but the amount of space they are using. If you want to exercise dominance make sure that you are using as much space as possible. When you are standing, place your hands on your hips with the elbows pointing out so you occupy more space. When you sit, stretch your legs out as far as possible. When you lean, walk, or find yourself in any other position, make sure that your body is occupying as much space as possible.

Women however, should exercise caution with body posing. More often than not, they will be labeled as taking on a less feminine role and/or of a less reputable position with open body language. She then would want to take a more closed pose but still exercise her dominance by using her body in other ways.

It also depends on the goal of the manipulator. If it is in a business environment, she would need to consider her audience. If she is in a group with many men and few women, a closed stance can be read as being defensive and she would want to avoid that at all costs. On the other hand, if she's in a more social setting with a balanced group around her, her closed body language could make her appear to be more open to a new relationship.

***Touching:*** There have been a number of studies that have shown how touching others while in conversation shows as more dominant. The act itself indicates that you are comfortable around them and are not intimidated or worried about invading another person's space. Of course, all of this is cultural and each environment needs to be taken into consideration. So, make sure that you understand the cultural dynamic of the people you're interacting with before you just decide to reach out a touch someone.

For women, touching men in any way could be perceived in the wrong way. If you're in a business setting avoiding even the slightest touch below the waistline. It is a powerful way to stimulate arousal. Again, women cannot use the power of touch as much as men without sending out the wrong vibes. And she should avoid touching strangers at all unless touching is viewed as acceptable in their culture.

***Holding Your Ground:*** When you're in a small or crowded space, it is normal to give a little to allow others to navigate. To assert your dominance, try to move a little as possible. In social settings, who moves for whom lets you know exactly who is the alpha.

- If you meet an old friend and they approach you, you are on the power side: try not to move.
- If you're in a group that needs something and others retrieve it, they are on the power side: move to accommodate them.
- If you're in a meeting in your office, you are the alpha: don't move.

This same rule can be applied in all types of settings. Whether in business or social settings these guidelines are based on how people naturally move when interacting with each other. We all instinctively know that we must move for the boss but be observant when you're in groups where there is no assigned rank to each person. This is where you can assert your dominance. People will automatically move for the person who acts more dominant or for the larger person.

***Eye Contact:*** Your eyes can also let people know that you're the top dog in the room. The longer you are able to hold eye-contact is usually an indication of your position in the setting. This is because the higher authority figures are quite comfortable maintaining eye contact with those under them. If you want to assert your dominance in a particular setting or group, don't look down.

If you do feel the need to break eye contact, make sure that you break it in the right way. If your eyes move up, it is read as a sign of dismissal. If they move to the side it is considered neutral and the two of you are on equal footing. However, if you break downwards it is always viewed as submissive, so never look down.

However, if you're a woman and looking to seduce, then looking down and then back up again is a clear signal that you want him. So, if that's your aim, then by all means, go for it.

***Comfort:*** The more comfortable you appear the more confidence you project. Nervousness sends a message of fear and anxiety. Try taking on a calmer and slower style to exude more confidence.

It is true that people who move fast and seem to exude energy can send out a message of fear, the person who moves slowly does not reflect any type of anxiety and appears to be much more grounded and in control. The message they send is that others can feel safe and relaxed around them.

There is also the concept of "locking in" where you use the most comfortable position you can in the setting. That could mean leaning against a bar or a railing, sitting on a stool, or leaning against a desk or a wall.

***Open Body Language:*** Asserting your dominance through open body language tells others that you are powerful. When your body is closed (hunched shoulders, crossed arms, and legs close together) it reflects an image of fear, anxiety, or unapproachable. However, when you display a more open body (arms out, legs apart, shoulders back) we appear dominant yet approachable. We let people know that we are confident and are in control.

***Relaxed Body Language:*** Also, a body that is relaxed sends a message of authority. When you show signs of comfort you appear more relaxed. Avoid sending displacement signals like scratching, touching your face or the back of your neck, wringing your hands, or unbuttoning the collar of your shirt. All of these signals show signs of nervousness and anxiety.

***Maintain Good Posture:*** Not only is good posture good for your health but it is also good for your image too. Your level of confidence is easily reflected in how you hold your body. When you stand erect and tall you exert a dominant and confident position but if you stand with your shoulders rounded, your head leaning forward (almost as in a permanent bow) you are taking a submissive position.

If you have been in this habit in the past, you need to start adjusting this stance as soon as possible. However, you need to be cautious and avoid over correcting. Extending your spine too far back can give you a swayback posture. Sticking your chest out too far will make you look cartoonish. Try making the adjustment in the mirror until you find the right balance.

***Do the Power Walk:*** There is some disagreement as to whether a power walk is fast or slow. A slow walk exudes more confidence as long as it represents your natural walking style. However, if you are moving slowly in a busy work environment it may send the message that you're lazy or unmotivated. By the same token, a fast walk can also exude confidence if done correctly. Still, it can be misconstrued as nervous or anxious depending on your environment.

So, while the speed of your walk can send a strong message, it is best to focus on how you walk. Make sure that as you move your shoulders move with you. A sway of the shoulders makes them look broader taking up more space. Use your arms with a smooth back and forth movement keeping them just slightly away from your body. When your arms are too close it is a sign of fear.

Keep the legs slightly apart allowing enough room for air to circulate and keeping the thighs from rubbing together.

Always stand up erect with your feet pointing slightly outward. You don't want to do it too much because it will give off an aire of disdain for those around you.

Keep you gaze staring straight ahead and focused to give you the appearance that your walk has a purpose.

***The Upward Nod:*** Make a habit of nodding with the chin thrusting upward rather than down. It gives you more of a rough appearance but only use it when necessary because in some crowds it can appear confrontational, which could cause more problems.

## How to Talk Like a Top Dog

Your physical positioning tells others you are confident and ready to tackle anything that comes your way. People will often defer to you when you display these physical body languages even if they don't understand why. But once they do come to you, it is important for your conversation to match the message that your body is sending out. How you express yourself will further solidify your dominance in any social dynamic.

***Lead the Conversation:*** When you speak, you must think about more than the words you choose to express your point of view. There are several variables that are important to regulating your conversation. As you assert your dominance, you need to be careful of your tone, tempo, subject matter, and who speaks the longest.

This is even more important when you are talking one on one with someone. In a group dynamic, there will always be a variety of characters to interact with however, when in a more private conversation where there are only two players, how you respond to questions and what you do will weigh heavily on who will have more dominance.

- **Tempo:** To exert dominance you need to control the speed of the conversation. You want to speak fast enough that you don't waste time but slow enough that you message is clearly understood. This means not only managing and regulating what you say, but your voice will set the tempo for the other person as well. In a group setting, it is your responsibility to make sure everyone is engaged in the same topic and on the same page. You also want to make sure to include everyone in the group. If you notice someone taking over the conversation, step in and cut them off with confidence.

In other words, you appoint yourself as the director of the conversation. Take control and gracefully interrupt when things start to go the wrong way. You could intervene in several ways.

*When one person is cut off by another:* "Wait a second." *Then address the person who was cut off,* "please, go ahead and finish your thought." *Or* "Let's hear what Janet has to say."

*When a person is talking too fast:* "Slow down, you're speaking to fast."

By taking the initiate to direct the conversation, you place yourself in a powerful dominant position and soon everyone in the group will be looking to you for direction even after the conversation has concluded and you've gone your separate ways.

- **Setting the Frame:** By the same token, directing the conversation also means deciding what's right to discuss. You decide what's fair, what's acceptable, and what's considered to be normal and appropriate conversation. The more power you exude at this stage the more people will respect and want to follow you.

- **Asking the Right Questions:** How you ask questions also plays a major role in asserting dominance. When engaging in conversation, always ask plenty of questions. In any conversational dynamic, the person who asks usually dominates the conversation and they person who answers is the subordinate.

- **Don't be Afraid to Offer Correction:** When you correct someone, you're making your power move. In essence, you are asserting your right to dictate the rules of the game. The more corrections you offer the higher your position of authority will be in their eyes. Only subordinates avoid correcting others or afraid of being viewed as taking a stand against authority.

  It is also a demonstration of your higher intellect, which is key in any dating dynamic. How you offer correction can make a difference too. For example, if you offer it in a way that shames the other person, they may see you as an authority but will lose respect for you. On the other hand, if you offer it with sincerity and with a feeling that you genuinely want to help, you will gain the respect you want.

- **Contradictions:** The same rules apply when you are contradicting another person. Whenever you are going to say something that is the exact opposite of what the other person believes, you are throwing down your dominance gauntlet. It is an extremely powerful move that if not done correctly could sever the entire relationship.

While this may be acceptable in some settings, those who have a higher social EQ understand just how risky this move is. Instead, they may just acknowledge the other person's point of view and then redirect the conversation subtly bringing in the correct answer without pointing out his or her error. This allows the other person to save face and garner you much more honor and respect than making an outright contradiction.

- **The Conclusion:** At the close of a conversation a leader will do a quick summary of what has been discussed. If you are not the leader but are trying to assert dominance the this would be the perfect time to step up and volunteer for this role. People will begin to see you as someone who can step up and be a good leader.

*Assertiveness:* It is important that you speak assertively. This means that you won't want to give up or relinquish your right to speak but instead make sure that everyone not only hears you but understands it too. There are several steps to accepting this role.

- **Make sure everyone understands:** As a leader your responsibility is not just to disseminate information but to make sure that all of your subordinates are clear on what is expected. You can verify this by asking questions like, "Are we clear?" "Do you understand?" or "Did you get it?" In some situations, you might ask them to repeat your instructions back to them so you know they fully grasp your expectations.

- **Always Expect an Answer:** In some situations, people will be reluctant to answer a question or concern you have raised. They may switch the subject or they may just pretend they didn't even hear the question. In some cases, they may even dismiss it as unimportant to the conversation. Never accept this. If you find someone who is reluctant or refuses to answer your question either repeat the question with a stronger tone that lets them know that you expect an answer or bring the conversation back around to the point of your discussion. Either way, never accept a non-answer to a direct question.
- **Repeat When Necessary:** If you find you are speaking in a group that may get too loud at times, the temptation is to raise your voice to make sure that you're heard. While this may work you run the risk of being seen as too aggressive rather than assertive. However, if you simply pause when the noise level gets too high and then repeat your message when the noise level drops again, you'll gain more respect.

You can also remind them of your official authority position and let them know that there is no other source for which to get the information you want to share with them. Make sure you have an assertive tone and the inflection reflects the kind of position you claim to have.

- **Avoid Being Verbally Aggressive:** Verbal aggression runs rampant on the political and business front. However, this doesn't mean you have to take that road. There is a difference between asserting your dominance and the use of verbal aggression. A person who is verbally aggressive will speak over people and at times literally rob them of their right to speak for themselves. They will cut people off or force them to be defensive in their remarks. These are strong-arm tactics where you are literally railroading the other person and forcing them into submission. While this will help you to be seen as an authority, you are instilling fear and intimidation to get what you want often even shaming them into accepting your position.

If you find yourself being attacked in this manner, don't go into the defensive mode. Instead, launch your own counterattack by reframing the subject in question or refuting their statements with your own evidence. As soon as you go on the defensive you automatically relinquish your power to them. Instead, stop his attack early on in the conversation. Match their own nastiness by pushing back with equal aggression or denying any accusations they may have made.

The launch your own counterattack, pointing out their hypocrisy or any errors in their argument. Remember, the power they gain from this encounter is only as strong as their accusations against you. Your goal is not to defend your argument but to rob them of their power. Don't take a stance on any position that it would be difficult to defend or prove. Work at showing a side that your opponent doesn't want seen and force him to get back to the truth as soon as possible. Winning a heated debate like that will earn you loads of points you would have to work even harder to achieve.

- **Ignore people:** By ignoring people, you show a lot of dominance. This is an important skill that is of high quality and can prove very valuable. You can prove your dominance by ignoring people's errors or when they take an action you don't approve of. Rather than blatantly pointing out their error, ignoring them is a silent way to show disapproval.

- **Say a lot with fewer words:** The most powerful people in the world are not always full of a lot of rhetoric. They don't mind people noticing them so they are calm in the face of social scrutiny. When they speak, they usually express themselves slowly and don't hesitate to pause to let the silence drive home their point.

When replying to another person, the general rule of thumb is to wait two seconds before speaking. Don't be afraid of the silence, it adds pressure to the other person and they are compelled to fill in the void.

- **Use Power Words:** Your speech should make good use of power words.
    - **Listen**
    - **I don't understand**
    - **Can you repeat that**
    - **Yes, that's right**
    - **No. That not right at all**
    - **Wrong!**
    - **You're mistaken.**
    - **And you're okay with that?**
    - **Before we continue, I need you to answer my question.**
    - **I don't want to talk about that now.**
    - **Tell me something more interesting.**
    - **Quiet! Silence!**
    - **The numbers speak for themselves.**

Whether you're speaking one on one or in a crowd, asserting dominance is all about projecting the right attitude. It is a very faint line that exists between being aggressive and being assertive, but if you can master these elements in asserting your dominance, you'll not only have a lot of people following you, you'll have earned their respect too.

## Dominant Behavior to Show Who's Boss

Showing dominance through behavior can be very similar to using body language. In fact, some of the methods here will overlap with those in how you present yourself physically. Spend some time observing people in power and you'll begin to see what social dominance really looks like.

**Take the Lead:** Clearly, taking the lead in any given situation can help you to assert your social dominance. Consider the impression you leave in others when you are:

- Walking. If you are going with a group, you'll notice how the more submissive people will begin to look around for someone to take the lead. As a leader, you don't wait, you just start walking. Try it and see just how many people will start to follow you.

   If you are new to a group, don't just jump ahead. Wait and see if they already have an established leader and if no one steps forward, then you can assert your position.

- Look for ways to protect those around you. This is a classic dominant role that exudes power and is deserving of respect. Protecting and caring for others could be simple gestures like offering someone a hand when they are trying to get out of their seat to defending their decision on a business project. This strategy has no downside. A strong leader who exercises care for those in his charge is a healthy way to get any kind of relationship off to a good start.

- Expect people to follow you. If people are not sure you're the leader it will be difficult for them to follow you, but simple gestures can help them along. For example, shaking someone's hand and placing the other on their back helps direct them to move in the direction you want them to go.

- Become a good guide: Take the initiative and invite others to join you whenever possible. Not only is this a powerful way to assert dominance people will automatically see you as a leader.

- Take the lead in small things. If the entire group sits, delay sitting for at least ten seconds before joining them. If you are invited inside, delay entering. You can tell them to take one second to enjoy the view or to answer a phone call. If you are in a position that dictates you must follow, do so in a nonchalant sort of way and avoid making any eye contact with them.

- Assign tasks: Whenever possible, give tasks to others. Delegating is a sign of authority. You will notice some people assign tasks even if they don't have any formal authority. If you are assigned a task, question the command. This will make the assigner have to defend his position. The more your challenge those in authority the more power you take for yourself. However, there will be times when someone does have the authority to give you a task. If this is the case, accept the assignment gracefully but continue to challenge tasks given from those who are not in an authority position to do so.

**Exert Social Pressure:** Creating tension within a social environment pressures other to comply. At times you can create tension even without a reason for it, just to assert your dominance.
Use intimidation with full frontal body language or loud aggressive tones in your voice to get less important individuals to cower in submission.

**Use Fewer Words:** Talking too much can be a sign that you are nervous or lack confidence. Rather than expressing every thought on your mind, let your facial expressions and body language communicate for you.

**Touching:** You can also show dominance through touching. In fact, just the act of touching alone can put you in a more dominant position. Studies have often shown that those who touch others are automatically viewed as more dominant. However, there is the right kind of touching and the wrong kind.
- **The Parental Touch:** Parental touches doesn't necessarily mean they are exclusive to parents and their children. A boss can use a parental touch and automatically push his charges into a more submissive role.
    - Patting them on the head
    - Pinching their cheek
    - Touching their face

    All of these touches indicate who is the parent and who is the child. They are also signaling that they are ready to take care of their subject and are ready to take charge.

**Follow the Pattern:** There is a distinct pattern of events that can carry you from the submissive one to the more dominant role in any type of relationship. You may start at the bottom rung of the ladder, then you move on to assertion, which will gradually slip you into a dominant role. The most effective role you can take is to follow the natural course of these patterns. The best ones to take an assertive role are those who are very good at handling those who are aggressive.

Part of that journey, however, is learning when to show aggression, punish, or intimidate. People who fall back on these dark habits when not needed usually earn the title of leader but not the respect due them. But there is a place for them in a number of interactions. Here are a few guidelines you need to follow.

- Slapping: This does not have to be a harsh type of slap that will leave your victim's cheeks burning. In fact, a light but threatening slap may be even more intimidating than outright brute force.
- Confiscating property: Picking up or taking another person's property is a very intimidating way to assert dominance. In essence, you are telling them that not only does their property belong to you but they do too. To fight back this approach, you can refuse to let them take your property or you can take theirs putting you both on equal footing.
- Territorial: Everyone feels territorial about something, but submissive people don't stand up for what they know is theirs. To assert your dominance, you will defend property that is your own with a strong sense of confidence.

**Command Attention:** Exerting a quiet sense of confidence always commands attention. There is no need to be flashy or bold in order to get people to follow you. While you can certainly take that route, just following the natural course of nature will have people gravitating to you with ease. Consider being helpful to those around you. By offering to fix problems, address needs, and protect those you want in your following, you will become a natural leader without too much effort.

Asserting your dominance may not be easy at first, especially if you're used to being in a more submissive position. But, if you continue to practice these simple techniques, you'll be surprised at just how fast you can move up in your role of becoming a master manipulator.

# Conclusion

Becoming a master manipulator is not as difficult as it may seem. It will take practice and commitment, and you won't master it overnight. Nothing you do well in life is ever easy, but if you stick with it through to the end you will inevitably yield positive results.

No doubt, you've heard a lot of things about manipulation. It's evil, it's dangerous, and it is demeaning, but there are both good and bad ways to view the practice. We live in a world of manipulators no matter where you look. The reality dictates that if you're not manipulating then there is a really good chance that you are being manipulated so you're going to be on one side of the coin whether you agree with it or not.

The question you really should be asking yourself is what kind of manipulator are you going to be. Parents manipulate their children as they mold them to become mature adults. Teachers manipulate their students to groom them for the future, and employers manipulate their charges to increase productivity. All of us have been manipulated in one way or another and we have all worked our magic on others. If your moral compass is triggered by this thought, then realize it is a matter of choice.

Becoming a master manipulator involves understanding how our thoughts and emotions work together. As your emotional intelligence grows so will our understanding in these areas. We've discussed how to build up our EQ and learn how to use it to identify our own emotions and those in others. This can become a powerful tool in our arsenal. Every master manipulator needs a good EQ. Without it, we will always struggle to get people to recognize us and give us what we want.

You also learned how to choose your target and the qualities that draw people to you. Everyone is not a prime target for manipulation and some can be much harder than others to convince. Especially in the beginning, you want to use the hooks listed in Chapter three to choose those who will be easier to convince. As you gain more experience, you can then try your skills on those harder and more challenging targets.

In Chapter Four we talked a great deal about body language. Learning how to read subtle cues can tell you a lot about a person and what they are thinking. Developing this skill can almost give you the power of mind reading. Learning about microexpressions and the way people walk will tell you much about what to expect and what you can ask from everyone around you.

Then we learned how to use several manipulation tools to help you get what you want. We started simply with some basic tactics that all people use and can easily be recognized. Applying the Six Laws of Persuasion can be very effective if you are well-informed about what they really are. Manipulation is a psychological game and the key to winning knowing where to position yourself to assert dominance over others. These tools are how you navigate this game.

So, whether you're looking to secretly manipulate your boss to do what you want or you're trying seduce someone into a romantic relationship the rules of the game are the same, you're just using different tools to accomplish your goals. Success can only come from asserting your dominance and staying the course.

Through the pages of this book, you have learned a lot about manipulation. No doubt, you will have to read some sections several times in order to get the full sense of them. But as you do, make sure to put them all into practice as soon as possible. This will help you to make faster progress. There will be times when you will fail miserably at your attempts to persuade others to do your bidding, but don't be discouraged; that is just part of the process. If you persist, it is just a matter of time before you can honestly say that you are truly a master manipulator.